UNDERSTANDING STEPFAMILIES

A practical guide for professionals working with blended families

T0368880

UNDERSTANDING STEPFAMILIES

A practical guide for professionals working with blended families

Lisa Doodson

Mc Graw Hill Education Open University Press

Open University Press
McGraw-Hill Education
8th Floor
338 Euston Road
London
NW1 3BT

email: enquiries@openup.co.uk
world wide web: www.openup.co.uk

and Two Penn Plaza, New York, NY 10121-2289, USA

First published 2016

A catalogue record of this book is available from the British Library

ISBN-13: 978-0-33-526478-0
ISBN-10: 0-33-526478-6
eISBN: 978-0-33-526479-7

Library of Congress Cataloging-in-Publication Data
CIP data applied for

Typeset by Aptara, Inc.

Fictitious names of companies, products, people, characters and/or data that may be used herein (in case studies or in examples) are not intended to represent any real individual, company, product or event.

Printed and bound by CPI Group (UK) Ltd, Croydon, CR0 4YY

PRAISE FOR THIS BOOK

"This book provides a comprehensive and solutions focused guide for all professionals seeking to understand the complexities of working with step family issues. Using well researched evidenced based theories, Dr Doodson delivers an essential manual filled with practical tips and tools that reflect the attitudes and methods necessary for negotiating the unique challenges and emotions experienced in step families.

As a step mother myself, I can testify that these methods provided our family with invaluable support and understanding at a difficult time and gave us the ideas and confidence to tackle some of the issues that were affecting day to day family life."

Susan Davis, Psychologist, mother and step-mother, UK

"Lisa Doodson's Understanding Stepfamilies *elegantly balances the accessible clarity required of a valuable 'how to' manual with the sort of summary of theoretical frameworks and relevant research that a reflexive practitioner will find very useful.*

Illustrated by engaging case studies that provide insights into the practical application of Integrated Stepfamily Therapy (IST) along with its tool box of road-tested exercises, I expect this book will become a well-thumbed reference for relationship practitioners who do the important work of supporting blended families in their varied and distinct forms."

Ewan Malcolm, Chief Executive,
Relate London North West, Board Member,
Family Mediation Council and College of Mediators

"The book achieves its goal to develop a better understanding of both the challenges and complexities of step families. I felt that the short snippets of case study were particularly helpful in demonstrating the variety of both the emotional and practical complications that can be experienced within step families, with no one family experiencing the same. The activities to be used with families provide a consistent, evidence-based approach that professionals can feel confident in using, allowing support for step families to get underway without delay.

I write this endorsement as a professional working with families, including many step families and as the biological parent in a step family."
Donna Briggs, Senior Co-ordinator Family Learning, UK

"This book brings a new clarity to the definition of the stepfamily – identifying key variables which impact their complexity and potential challenges. Lisa's approach – Integrated Stepfamily Therapy (IST) – recognises the importance of truly understanding the uniqueness of the stepfamily and offering a range of support as couples seek to develop their family unit. Lisa combines sound theory with practice in the form of case studies, comprehensive tables of definitions as well as easy-to-use toolkits. Definitely the 'go-to guide' for professionals working with blended families as well as a tremendous resource and ray of hope for any step-parent!"
Genevieve Loaker, CEO Mosaic Lives (and step-mum)

CONTENTS

PREFACE

Having spent the past 10 years researching and studying stepfamilies, not to mention being part of a stepfamily myself for more than 15 years, I feel well equipped and well placed to write authoritatively on the subject. This book is intended to extend the range of techniques and resources professionals can draw on in their work with blended families.

Yet, despite my experience and knowledge in the subject, writing this book has been an interesting challenge. Even the title has caused a great deal of debate – should we be using the term 'stepfamily' or 'blended family', and is there a difference between the terms? You will have noticed that in both the title and the opening paragraph I have used the terms stepfamily and blended family. In doing so, I want to signify that the terms are interchangeable. Stepfamily is the most well used and well-understood name to describe a family involving children from a prior relationship, however it is often associated with negative connotations – the wicked stepmother of fairy tales, being one such example. Family professionals have in recent years sought to find a more palatable replacement, and 'blended families' has become a term that is frequently used. However, while professionals are becoming more used to referring to blended families, the general public are still more familiar with the term stepfamily, and may not recognise themselves as blended families. I think it less important what name we use, than that we focus on the common issues that these types of family face. As stepfamilies become more common I believe that the stigma that was once apparent is becoming less so as both numbers and awareness increases.

I began researching stepfamilies driven by my own change in family circumstances and a desire to understand more fully the wider challenges of stepfamilies. In 2006, I conducted the largest study on stepmothers in the UK, involving more than 250 from across the UK. The research identified a number of alarming differences between step-mothers and biological mothers. Stepmothers for example showed significantly higher anxiety and depression than biological mothers; they relied on more ineffective coping mechanisms; they had poorer social support and an overall lower quality of life (Doodson, 2014; Doodson and Davies, 2014). Follow-up interviews with the women highlighted some of the common frustrations they experienced. For example, some struggled to understand their role in the new family and had different views from their partner. Many stepmothers, particularly those who had no biological children of their own, also found it incredibly difficult to know how to behave with their partner's children. When should they discipline? When should they step back? And the relationship with the biological mother was incredibly complex, in terms of their expectations and emotions. Many of the stepmothers wanted recognition from the biological mother for the role they played in helping parent their stepchildren, while others felt that they were doing a better job than the biological mother and were often quick to criticise. In general the women were frustrated in a role that they felt was largely unrecognised and not valued by either the biological mother or society in general. I think one of the most interesting and salient moments for me was the relief these women found in finally being able to express their views. They recognised that the research had come too late to help them and their families, however they were willing to take part in the hope that they could help others in the future. Almost without exception they told me of their frustration in not knowing where to turn to for help. There were no role models or societal rules for stepfamilies.

For me, the value of any research is in its dissemination and application in the real world. While understanding more about common issues, emotions and behaviour helps inform us, the real value is in developing interventions that address the underlying issues. Based on my findings from the primary research, and using pre-existing stepfamily research, I developed a series of workshops and training programmes for couples in stepfamilies as well as for professionals working with stepfamilies. My work over recent years has been spent delivering and evaluating these courses and also in working individually with couples, either using brief therapy or mediation techniques, which I describe in the book.

Writing this book has of course made me question and test my approach. There have been other well-respected experts who have written eloquently and intelligently about therapy for stepfamilies – these are discussed and evaluated in Chapter 3. So what does this book do differently? I believe this is the first book to consider an integrated approach to stepfamilies, recognising that different interventions may be appropriate for different types of blended families. I have also introduced a number of case studies throughout the book that help to illustrate the approach and provide practical support for professionals and a range of tools for them to draw on in their support of stepfamilies. These include exercises that can be used with clients to support the sessions. I want to inspire readers to consider offering clients a broader choice of support, and hence reach and help more stepfamilies.

Stepfamilies are the fastest-growing family type in society. We need to ensure that we understand their needs and provide support that targets their unique difficulties. In this way I hope we can help more families become successful, happy and healthy family units, providing a safe and secure environment in which children can thrive and develop. I sincerely hope this book begins to enable that change.

Dr Lisa Doodson

ACKNOWLEDGEMENTS

I would like to thank my colleagues, Paul Randolph and Desa Markovich, for their support of this project. Their advice and encouragement have been invaluable.

I would also like to thank my husband, Mike, for having the patience to review numerous drafts of the book and for keeping me motivated through to the end!

I would like to express my heartfelt thanks to Barbara Bloomfield for her time and patience in reviewing drafts of the book and also for providing a range of resources that practitioners can draw on when working with blended families. Her support has been invaluable.

Finally, I'd like to thank Regent's University London, who generously gave me the time and space to write this book. I am grateful for their continued support.

1 DEFINING A STEPFAMILY

Stepfamily is a well used but often misunderstood term. What do we mean when we say we are part of a stepfamily or work with stepfamilies in our role as helping practitioners? The 2001 UK census was the first UK census to allow the identification of stepfamilies, defining a stepfamily as a family where at least one child belongs to only one member of the married or cohabiting couple. In the 1990s, a similar census in the US recognised stepfamilies, however only where the couple were married. Children of unmarried stepparents were typically classified as living in single-parent families. Stepfamilies are now a large and integral part of our society, and our inability to measure their number can only impede our ability to understand and support them. In today's society we need to adopt a much broader and all-encompassing definition of a stepfamily or blended family.

This introductory chapter therefore defines our current understanding of stepfamilies and addresses the following questions.

- How many stepfamilies are there in the UK?
- What is a 21st-century definition of a stepfamily?
- What are the differences between biological and stepfamilies, and how might these inform our therapeutic approach?

What is a stepfamily?

Historically, stepfamilies were formed when adults remarried and one or both had children from a previous marriage. However, social and demographic shifts – including the growth in the number of women having children outside of marriage, an increase in couples cohabiting rather than marrying, increases in non-residential parental involvement and shared physical custody of children after divorce – have caused many stepfamily researchers to re-evaluate what constitutes a stepfamily (Bumpass, Raley and Sweet, 1995; Stewart, 2005) and to adopt a much more inclusive definition. De'Ath (1997) suggests that a more appropriate stepfamily definition may be as follows:

> A stepfamily is a family created by two adult partners, one or each of whom already has a child from a previous relationship; the offspring from a former marriage ended by separation, death or divorce; a former cohabitation or extra marital affair. A stepfamily may include resident stepchildren or partially resident children who live primarily with their other parent and children of the two adults, who are half siblings to the stepchildren. The stepfamily relationship exists, even when the adults and children have not met each other or live together, and extends to grandparents, aunts, uncles and cousins.

(p. 267)

It is important to consider not only the impact of the immediate family members on the development of the new family unit, but also the extended family of grandparents, aunts and uncles, siblings and even friends. Researchers now recognise that couples form stepfamilies whether they have formalised their relationship with marriage or are simply living together. However, I believe it's important to ask further questions in order to truly clarify what we now understand to be a stepfamily.

I recently had an interesting debate with a colleague who is also a stepmother. Her own experiences of being part of a stepfamily have been nothing but positive. She and her husband both have a good relationship with their ex partners to the extent that they all attend significant family events such as weddings, graduations and christenings together. They both have children from prior relationships and close bonds have developed between everyone. The children, who are now all adults, all get on extremely well with one another and think of themselves as siblings. Both adults love and care for their children and stepchildren equally. My colleague was puzzled that we continue to label stepfamilies as such and, based on her own experiences, argued that they are simply a different type of family and we should not stigmatise them by differentiating them from biological families. While this is a valid argument when things are going well, I don't believe it helps stepfamilies who are struggling to cope with the specific difficulties associated with this family structure. It also perpetuates the myth that all stepfamilies experience problems. Identifying good role models, of 'successful' stepfamilies could potentially help those experiencing more difficulties.

Stepfamily growth and definition

As a result of changing family patterns, stepfamilies now represent the fastest-growing family type in the UK (Economic and Social Research Council (ESRC), 2004). Despite this, accurate statistics for stepfamily populations continue to be very difficult to define. Demographers generally rely on a 'household' as the unit of measurement. This holds true in both the UK (Office for National Statistics (ONS), 2001) and the US (US Census Bureau, 2005), where a household reflects the individuals who live there on a permanent basis only. The demographic definition of a family or stepfamily follows the Western tradition of thinking of families as being contained within a single household (Cherlin and Furstenberg, 1994). Households form neat units for counting individuals and their relationships. However this definition omits many stepfamily relationships, which by necessity span multiple households.

Let's take the example of **Sue and Dave**. They were married for five years and had two children together. They subsequently divorced, with the children living with their mother but regularly visiting their father for weekends and holidays. Sue continues to live on her own with the children, while Dave found a new partner and started to cohabit. Using the household rule, Sue's household would be classified as a single-parent household and Dave would be classified as a couple household because the children are classed as residing with Sue. Dave and his new partner would not be counted in the statistics of stepfamilies as the children 'reside' predominantly with their mother. They would be one of the hidden statistics of stepfamilies.

The current definition therefore excludes many stepfamilies, particularly those that care for their stepchildren on a shared or part-time basis. While women are still usually granted primary care of children following a divorce, in both the US (Cancian and Meyer, 1998) and in the UK (Ferri and Smith, 1998), the predominant residential stepfamily involves the biological mother and stepfather (ONS, 2001; US Census Bureau, 2005). Non-residential stepfamilies are therefore largely step-mother led, with the majority of these families being excluded from national statistics in both the UK and US.

According to national records, there are 473,000 stepfamilies in the UK (ONS, 2011). This compares against approximately 700,000 stepfamilies in the UK, according to the ONS, ten years earlier in 2001. Anecdotal evidence would suggest it unlikely that the number of stepfamilies has reduced in the past ten years so there is clearly an inherent difficulty in adequately capturing stepfamily statistics. In North America figures taken from the 2000 census, show that almost 4.4 million stepchildren (8 per cent of all children) live in stepfamilies (Kreider, 2003). The census also recognises that it may have identified only a proportion of stepchildren given the fact that families may have been incorrectly categorised depending on whether the biological or stepparent completed the census form (Kreider, 2003). More recent census figures (US Census Bureau, 2005) suggest that the number of children residing in stepfamilies has grown significantly, with 12.2 million children now residing with a stepparent, stepsibling or half sibling, representing 17 per cent of all children.

The Australian Bureau of Statistics (ABS) defines a family as 'usually resident in the same household' (2004, p.71). While this makes the number of families more measurable, it fails to differentiate between family types, meaning there is little clarity on stepfamily numbers (de Vaus, 2004). The ABS reports the current proportion of stepfamilies as 10.6 per cent of all couple families, representing a 50 per cent increase over 10 years from 7 per cent in 1996 (ABS, 1998). Clearly, if part-time and non-residential families were also taken into account, these figures would be significantly higher. Additional international data are difficult to find. Teachman and Tedrow (2008, in Pryor, 2008) suggest that the percentages of stepfamilies in France and Sweden were 8 per cent in 1999 and 9 per cent in 2002, respectively, compared with 10 per cent in 2004 for the UK and 13 per cent in 2000 in the US, with the higher rates in the US being driven largely by the higher rates of marriage and divorce.

International statistics therefore suggest that approximately 10 per cent of all families are now stepfamilies, although we could argue that this figure is artificially low, as it largely ignores part-time and non-residential stepfamilies. Visibility of stepfamilies in society is further compounded however by issues associated with the stepfamily image. Many stepfamily members, perhaps deliberately or possibly unknowingly, fail to recognise their stepfamily status (Visher and Visher, 1996; Berger, 1998).

Emma and Steve came to see me recently. Steve had a 12-year-old son from a previous relationship and they had an 18-month-old baby together. There were issues in integrating the family and both adults were eager to find ways of addressing the ongoing issues. When I asked Emma to describe her family, she explained that it consisted of herself and Steve and their baby, and that Steve also had a son from a previous relationship. She told me that she felt they were a biological family – as they had a son together – and did not relate to the stepfamily term in any way. To her, the term 'stepfamily' related only to couples who had children from prior relationships – not children together. Consequently, the majority of her friends were completely unaware that Steve had another child, or that Emma was a stepmother. Emma explained that she was now embarrassed to tell people after 'pretending to be normal' for so long. The family had recently been invited to a friend's wedding and this was causing Emma much anxiety as only their baby had been invited. Steve's older child would be with them for the weekend and Emma was struggling to know what to do – she would either have to find someone to care for him on the day of the wedding or she would have to explain to her friend that her stepson was staying with them and ask if he could join them at the wedding.

After some discussion, Emma agreed that she would talk to her friend and explain the situation. Of course her friend was surprised to learn about Emma's stepson but was more than happy for him to join the celebration.

Emily, a participant in a recent stepparenting workshop, described her stepson as 'her partner's child' and did not recognise herself as a stepmother. She felt that as they were not married she couldn't be classified as a stepmother. It's not uncommon even for different members of the household to hold different views of their family structure. Take Rachel and John, for example.

Rachel needed help with a number of stepfamily-related issues and felt attending a workshop might be useful. However she was worried that it was aimed only at what she called 'blended stepfamilies'. I asked her to tell me what she felt a blended stepfamily was and why that wasn't relevant to her. She believed that a blended stepfamily consisted of both adults having children from previous relationships. Her husband, **John,** *had two children from a previous relationship when they first met and they had a joint child who was now a year old. Since the birth of their child the couple had started to struggle with problems in their own relationship and between the various children. They were both eager to find help in dealing with the difficulties. Rachel identified with being a stepmother and hence being in a stepfamily, however John felt that, as he had fathered all the children, he was in a biological family.*

These examples illustrate the difficulty in both recognising and accurately 'counting' stepfamilies. Not only do we struggle as a society to define a stepfamily but also individuals often fail to identify themselves with the definition. Thus stepfamilies are often unacknowledged and unrecognised in society. It could be argued that a general negative perception of stepfamilies and stepparents can lead to a reluctance to identify oneself as part of a stepfamily and this, in turn, will perpetuate their under-representation. When coupled with the statistical under-representation of stepfamilies it becomes clear that stepfamilies continue to be a hidden statistic in society.

Does the couple have to live together?

I have met many couples in recent years who have decided for largely practical reasons not to live together. Often these couples have had large families and it was impractical to find or afford a home for all the children. Sometimes, the couples were also reluctant to make any changes in living arrangements to avoid impacting their children's education. While one could argue that these couples were not part of a stepfamily, many of the issues they faced were related to stepfamily dynamics. For example, if the couple spend a significant time together at each other's homes, the issue of discipline will be raised. Their time together or holidays may well be impacted by ex partners who change

Table 1.1 Family relationship definitions

Name	Definition
Biological family	The name used to define couples who have only biological children; often individuals refer to these as natural, real or intact families (see below)
Biological parent/ mother/father	These terms relate to adults who have children that are genetically their own
Natural parent/ mother/father Real parent/father/ mother Intact family parent/ father/mother	I would advise against using these terms and encourage clients (and practitioners!) to use the term 'biological' when referring to families that contain only biologically related children; the terms 'natural' and 'real' imply by default that any other family type is therefore 'unnatural' or not real; similarly the term 'intact' has negative connotations
Stepfamily	The name used to define families that include children from previous relationships of either or both adults
Blended family/ reconstituted family	Alternative terms to describe stepfamilies, which have been introduced over recent years; however one could argue that they do not define the nature of a stepfamily – the aim is not to 'blend' these new families but to give them their own unique identity, which brings with it its own challenges; calling stepfamilies 'blended' or 'reconstituted' often places unrealistic demands on them
Stepmother	A dictionary definition assumes that a stepmother is the wife of a man who has children from a previous relationship; for the purposes of counselling and therapy, a woman should be considered to be a stepmother if her partner (regardless of marital status) has children from a previous relationship; the reality is that women dating men with prior children are effectively taking on the role of stepmother in some shape or form, regardless of marital status and living arrangements
Stepfather	Similarly, the dictionary definition of a stepfather is a man who is married to a woman who has children from a prior relationship; in the same way as for a stepmother, I recommend that therapists assume this relationship exists for couples where the women has children from a prior relationship, regardless of marital status and living arrangements

(continued)

Table 1.1   Family relationship definitions (*continued*)

Name	Definition
Stepfather-led stepfamily	Defines a stepfamily where only the woman has children from a previous relationship, hence there is a biological mother and a stepfather in the household; the couple may or may not have biological children together
Stepmother-led stepfamily	Defines a stepfamily where only the man has children from a previous relationship, hence there is a biological father and a stepmother in the household; the couple may or may not have biological children together
Complex stepfamily	Defines a stepfamily where both adults have children from prior relationships; the couple may or may not have additional biological children together
Simple stepfamily	Defines a stepfamily where only one adult in the family has children from a previous relationship; this may be either a stepfather- or stepmother-led family; the couple may or may not have additional biological children together
Residential stepchildren	This term relates to stepchildren who live for the majority of the time with the stepfamily; it is also the family unit where the children legally reside; often stepchildren divide their time between their biological parents and, frequently, they spend a larger proportion of their time at one household, which is termed their residential home; even for children who share their time equally between biological parents there will be one household that is legally defined as their main home
Non-residential stepchildren	This term relates to stepchildren who live for the minority of the time within the family unit; they often reside with their other biological parent and visit the other stepfamily home; the amount of time non-residential stepchildren spend in this household can vary from 50 per cent of the time to occasional visits throughout the year, however the term does not differentiate between them
Siblings	Defines children who share the same two biological parents
Half siblings	Defines children who share only one biological parent
Stepsiblings	Defines children who have no biological parents in common, however one child's biological parent is in a relationship with the other children's biological parent
Mutual children	This term defines children who are the biological children of both adults within the stepfamily

arrangements or need support with childcare. It is therefore important that practitioners consider whether a couple might be experiencing issues related to stepfamily dynamics even when they don't present as such.

Do the stepchildren live with the couple all the time?

In the majority of stepfamilies, children will spend some time away from the household, visiting their absent other parent. Historically, when couples separated or divorced, residency was frequently given to the mother, with the children visiting the father regularly, however while this remains the case for many couples, in recent years it has become more common for couples to share the care of their children, with the children spending equal time at both homes. However, regardless of the amount of time children spend with or apart from a parent, if their biological parent has a new partner, this new family unit should be considered a stepfamily.

Are the stepchildren adults and live away from home?

In the UK, national statistics will consider a family unit a stepfamily only if the children are under the age of 18 and live in the family home. However couples who have adult children from previous relationships face the same pressures as those with younger children. An example of this is Kim, who came to see me recently.

Kim had been living with Rob for seven years. Kim had no children of her own and Rob had two adult children from a previous marriage who were currently living with his ex partner in America. For the majority of the time Kim and Rob lived as a childless couple, however once a year, over the summer, Rob's 19-year-old son would come to visit. He would stay with the couple for several weeks, during which time Kim felt an outsider as Rob enjoyed catching up with his son.

Kim came to see me as she was struggling to cope with her feelings of frustration, jealousy and resentment. She was ashamed of her feelings as she recognised how hard it was for Rob not seeing his children for the majority of the year, however the contrast between their life as a couple and with Rob's son was difficult for her to cope with. Kim felt that, when Rob's son came to stay, her position changed in the family and she felt very much an outsider. Naturally Rob wanted to spend as much time as possible with his son but this came at the expense of his relationship with Kim. Rob felt that Kim should understand and be more accepting of the situation. Every time Kim spoke to Rob about her feelings they ended up arguing, with Rob accusing Kim of being selfish and not welcoming his son into their home. Kim began to dread the summer months, recognising the impact the summer would have on her relationship with Rob. While Rob saw his son for only six weeks in a year, that period was beginning to define his relationship with Kim.

My work with the couple was first based on helping them understand each other's perspectives. Rob felt guilty that he couldn't be a father to his son for much of the year and tried to compensate for this over the summer, spending as much time as possible with him. He thought that Kim would understand this and give them space to build their relationship. Kim did understand but expected Rob to put her first occasionally while his son was staying with them. It transpired that every evening Rob stayed up into the early hours of the morning watching sport with his son. Kim would go to bed on her own and then leave for work, barely seeing her partner or stepson. Rob also avoided making any arrangements with Kim that excluded his son over the summer; consequently the couple didn't have any time together.

I suggested that perhaps they could make a few small changes that might make the summer more enjoyable for all three of them. Rob needed to recognise that Kim was being excluded from his relationship with his son. I recommended that they spent some time each week doing an activity that they could all enjoy. This would help create memories for them all to share and draw on. However, it was also important to create some time for Kim and Rob during the summer and I suggested a date night once a week. Rob was reluctant to leave his son out but was willing to try in order to save his relationship with Kim. I explained that I was sure his son would understand and would probably welcome some time on his own in the house occasionally. I also thought it was important that Kim felt included in the plans that

Rob made every year with his ex partner regarding his son's visit. Kim felt that the arrangements were something that took place exclusively within the former biological family unit, from which she was excluded. I recommended that Rob talk to Kim about the plans for the summer visit so that they could make plans together as a couple. This would reduce her anxiety about the forthcoming visit and help her to see the visit in a more positive light.

This case study illustrates that stepchildren – regardless of their age or physical location – can have a huge impact on the couple relationship. As a greater number of older couples are now choosing to separate and divorce this issue is likely to become more common. It is therefore important to recognise the impact of adult stepchildren on a relationship, even though the couple may not present as a typical stepfamily unit.

What if one biological parent has died?

Historically, stepfamilies were more likely to form following the death of one of the biological parents. Nowadays, stepfamilies are more likely to form following separation or divorce. However many stepfamilies are still formed following the death of a biological parent and it is important to recognise the effect this may have on the new family unit. One of the frequent sources of stress for stepfamilies is the interaction with the absent biological parent. Many couples secretly wish that the other biological parent were no longer around, believing this would make their lives easier and more closely resemble those of biological families. However the reality is that, whether the absent biological parent is physically or emotionally absent, they will always have an impact on the stepfamily.

Stepfamilies formed when the absent biological parent has died have more control over their family unit. They no longer have to consult with another adult, or compromise with arrangements or access. However, they have to cope with the emotional loss to the child or children of their other parent. Children frequently resent a stepparent trying to replace their parent, and the surviving parent often tries to compensate for their children's loss. Sometimes this is reflected in excessive generosity or in the inability to discipline their children. Stepparents can therefore feel frustrated and excluded from this tight biological unit. A recent case study illustrates these pressures well.

Paul and Sonia had been together for a year. Paul had a daughter aged 12 and Sonia a son aged 4. The couple still lived apart but were considering moving in together as a family, however they felt that Paul's daughter was dictating the pace. Paul's wife died three years earlier. Her death had been unexpected and had naturally left Paul and their daughter devastated. During the time since his wife's death, Paul had done his best to maintain consistency and security for his daughter. They had stayed in the same family home and she attended the same school. Paul's daughter had coped relatively well, her grades were good and she had a close circle of friends at school. Paul explained that he had come to rely on his daughter to carry out her share of household tasks. They'd become a tight partnership, holding the home together between them. As Paul slowly recovered, he decided to join a dating website and even talked to his daughter about his plans. However once he met Sonia and they started to spend time together, he found that his daughter became more difficult. When he made plans for them to spend time together she would make excuses not to go, forcing Paul to cancel the plans. When Sonia came round, Paul's daughter would be rude to her and exclude her from conversations or activities with her father. When I spoke to Paul, it became evident that he had not told his daughter that Sonia was his girlfriend, instead choosing to tell her that she was just a friend.

Paul and Sonia understood that his daughter would feel nervous and possibly jealous of any new relationship but they wanted to know how they could help her learn to accept his new relationship and not feel threatened by Sonia. I felt the key was in changing Paul's behaviour. Following the death of his wife, Paul and his daughter had formed a tight bond, sharing in their grief. They had helped each other recover, but during this time Paul had also leaned quite heavily on his daughter: he had expected her to take on many of the household chores, which she had initially been happy to do, however over time it became clear that she resented these responsibilities and wanted to be treated in the same way as her school friends. This change in role had also changed her perceived status in the family. She became more like an adult in the relationship and as such felt she had more control in the family unit. As Sonia joined the unit, she sensed this changing and fought to assert and maintain her control through refusing to accept plans her father and Sonia made.

I suggested that Paul needed to clarify both his daughter's and Sonia's roles in the family. His daughter desperately wanted to be like her peers, with none of the adult responsibilities, however she also wanted to maintain her elevated status in the family unit. Paul needed to take away some of the mundane responsibilities he had pushed onto his daughter so that she could enjoy the transition to teenager in the same way as her friends. I also recommended that he took the time to talk to his daughter to explain that he was in a romantic relationship with Sonia and that he wanted them to spend more time together. I suggested that he should involve his daughter more – making her aware of plans in advance and making it clear when he expected her to be involved. While some events would be non-negotiable, for others he might want to give her the choice of whether she wanted to be invited or not.

Stepfamilies formed through separation, divorce or death all experience issues related to the development of the new family, however there are distinct differences between them, which should be recognised by practitioners.

Differences between stepfamilies and biological families

Stepfamilies and biological families have a number of inherent differences. So while many individuals dislike the term stepfamily and would rather be considered as biological families, this does not help the development of the new family and the integration of its members. Table 1.2 identifies some of these key differences, and the section that follows explores these further and identifies implications for therapy.

Biological families are formed when a couple has children together. In stepfamilies, the order is reversed, with children preceding the couple relationship. This change in dynamic can make it more difficult for the couple relationship to develop, with the additional demands and constraints of the children from previous relationships. In addition to this, the couple also has to negotiate pre-existing relationships with ex partners and extended family members, all of whom continue to influence the new couple and developing stepfamily.

In part due to these additional stresses and strains, the roles within a stepfamily are far more ambiguous than those within biological families. There is a lack of clarity and consistency in the roles of stepparents in the newly formed family unit. Perhaps one of the most quoted articles

Table 1.2   Key differences between biological and stepfamilies

	Biological family	Stepfamily
Differences related to couples in biological and stepfamilies	The couple relationship was established before the children were born	The parent–child relationship was established before the couple relationship The biological parent can feel torn between their children and their new partner
	The couple are a distinct unit with existing links to ex partners	The couple often have complex relationships with the other biological parents and extended relations
	Biological roles are clear and unambiguous	Stepparent roles are highly ambiguous and develop over time
Differences related to children in biological and stepfamilies	They are members of only one household	They are often members of two households
	Their family position is fixed	Sibling order can change between households
	Loyalty conflicts are rare	Children can often feel torn between their biological parents or between their stepparent and parent
	There is usually an equal parental relationship in terms of discipline	Discipline is often difficult for stepparents in the early stages of the relationship
Differences related to family in biological and stepfamilies	The family develops and members bond naturally over time	The couple forms an instant family, which may or may not be accepted by the individuals
	There are blood ties between the adults and all children	Some of the relationships exist only due to the couple relationship and cease to exist if the relationship ends
	Family relationships are generally close between all members	Relationships may be quite distant, particularly in the early stages
	History and traditions evolve, with all members sharing in the development	There is little or no shared history between members; this has to develop over time
	They are accepted and understood within society	They are poorly understood within society; no clear social norms

(continued)

Table 1.2   Key differences between biological and stepfamilies (*continued*)

	Biological family	Stepfamily
	Joint finances are confined to one household	Finances often have to be divided between households
	There is a clearly defined legal status	The legal status is unclear, the stepparent generally has no legal relationship with the stepchildren

on stepfamilies was that written by Cherlin in 1978. He suggested that remarriage was an incomplete institution because there was an absence of guidelines and norms for roles, and it was this that contributed to greater stress for stepfamilies as they tried to develop their own rules and roles in their new families.

In daily life we are surrounded by models of families with two adults and their children, or single-parent families, both equally portrayed in the media. But there are few examples of stepfamilies and even fewer *successful* stepfamilies. As roles within stepfamilies are so vague, it's difficult for stepparents to assess whether they are succeeding in their roles, leading to ever increasing confusion and anxiety. As a consequence some stepparents feel frustrated in trying to fill a largely undefined role for which they have no training. Often the situation can be worse for stepmothers than stepfathers as they are more often the part-time stepparent and as such have fewer socially accepted role prescriptions than stepfathers.

There is also some evidence that remarried couples may possess poorer conflict resolution and problem-solving skills than couples in first marriages (Larson and Allgood, 1987), however, whether this means that remarried couples are typically deficient in their use of coping strategies or whether they are merely overwhelmed by the degree of stress in their lives is unclear. My own research has suggested that stepparents engage in more negative or maladaptive coping strategies. These are typically related to mental or behavioural disengagement, where individuals either stop thinking about a particular stressor or give up trying to cope, having overwhelming feelings of helplessness (Lazarus and Folkman, 1984). For example, they may daydream or engage in other activities in order to take their mind off their problems. Alternatively, they just stop trying and admit to themselves that they can't solve the problems. These behaviours are particularly prevalent in stepparents who are struggling to cope with their stepchildren. The following case study illustrates this.

Alison, *a stepmother with two stepdaughters under the age of 10, was experiencing a number of difficulties following the birth of her first baby when I first met her. She admitted that while in the past she had tried to engage with the girls, more recently she had felt the situation was hopeless and was now finding ways of avoiding them when they came to visit. As soon as the girls arrived she would put her coat on and pretend that she had to go somewhere. In reality she was just making excuses to avoid them. However, the effect of this was simply to increase her feelings of isolation and withdrawal from the family. I was able to make her realise that she was simply avoiding the problem and needed to find more positive ways of coping. I encouraged Alison to talk to her partner about her feelings and, together, find ways of spending time as a family with all the children. However, it was also important that Alison felt she had some time on her own when she could 'escape' if she was finding this difficult.*

The practitioner's role is critical in identifying the overuse of maladaptive coping strategies and suggesting alternative coping options. Often when individuals understand how their behaviour is affecting their wellbeing, they are more than willing to make the necessary changes.

Table 1.3 highlights a range of recognised coping styles. While some are known to be generally associated with more positive outcomes, others have been found to correlate with less positive outcomes, particularly if individuals engage in these in favour of alternative approaches. Individuals who rely on more so-called negative coping mechanisms should therefore be encouraged over time to rely on alternative styles. It should be noted, however, that it is normal for any of us to turn to negative or maladaptive styles from time to time; the issue is when we come to rely on this approach too heavily or at the expense of other, more effective coping styles.

By asking clients how they cope with a particular stressor, practitioners can establish if they are relying too heavily on negative coping styles. Once you've identified trends, encourage clients to turn to more positive styles as these are more likely to lead to better outcomes, both for the individual and the family.

Table 1.3 Alternative coping mechanisms

Negative or maladaptive coping mechanisms	Example statement	Positive coping mechanisms	Example statement
Mental disengagement – individuals engage in other activities in order to stop thinking about the problem	'I daydream about being a "normal" family'	Social support – individuals seek practical or emotional support from family and friends	'I talk to my best friend about things. She was in a stepfamily so really seems to understand how I feel'
Behavioural disengagement – individuals reduce the amount of effort they put in to addressing the problem or give up entirely; it is closely related to helplessness	'I have a terrible relationship with my stepdaughter. I don't know how to fix it so I've stopped trying'	Active coping – individuals take steps to remove or reduce the effects of the problem	'I know I haven't got the best relationship yet with my stepson but I am really trying to make things better. Last week we spent time at the park – just the two of us'
Venting of emotions – individuals have a tendency to focus on the stress, and frequently ventilate their feelings	'I just get really upset with my partner. He doesn't understand why I find it so hard but I can't explain'	Humour – use of humour to deal with the stressor and make it more manageable	'We're always having to reorganise our plans due to my partner's ex – she is so disorganised. But if we couldn't laugh about it I think I'd cry!'
		Acceptance – accepting the reality of the situation	'At first I just wanted to be "normal", then I realised there is no real "normal". I've accepted we have our own challenges and now we're trying to make our family the best we can be'

(continued)

Table 1.3   Alternative coping mechanisms (*continued*)

Negative or maladaptive coping mechanisms	Example statement	Positive coping mechanisms	Example statement
		Planning – thinking about how to cope with the stressor	'Holidays are so difficult to agree but now we make sure we plan a long way ahead so that the dates are in the diary. It's made life so much easier for us'
		Positive reinterpretation and growth – thinking about the stressor in positive terms, about what can be learned from the experience	'Being part of a stepfamily is really challenging at times, but I think it has made me more aware of how people feel. I think I'm much better now at empathising'

A good social support network, made up of family and friends, is essential to our wellbeing. There is a well-reported and consistent correlation between social support and emotional wellbeing, with an absence of social support a reliable predictor of depression (e.g. Brown, Harris and Hepworth, 1994). A strong social support network can also act as a buffer between stressful life events and symptoms of stress (Zimet *et al.*, 1988). Research has found evidence that stepfamilies often experience poorer social support from family and friends than biological families. This seems to be particularly significant if both partners were previously in relationships (Booth and Edwards, 1992). Individuals in remarriages tend to be involved in fewer social groups that can provide support (Forste and Heaton, 2004) and receive support from fewer members in their family of origin (Kurdek, 1989).

Choosing to have children is a major decision in anyone's life, but one that is well understood and recognised in society. When a woman becomes pregnant she finds herself with a whole new support network, guiding and helping her cope with the new challenges ahead. Couples start to attend antenatal classes, where they can meet other couples in the same situation, together with professionals who can guide and care for them. In contrast, a stepfamily receives no such support. There are no groups to join or support offered. Individuals who did not have children of their own before becoming stepparents often find this transition extremely difficult and feel they have no one to turn to.

Rhona came to see me a short time after marrying and moving in with her partner. Her partner's children lived with them part-time and she had no children of her own. Rhona was suffering from mild depression and anxiety, and was finding it very hard to cope with the changes in her life since marrying. When I started to talk to Rhona, I discovered that, prior to meeting her husband, she had lived and worked in a different part of the country, but had moved with her partner so they could be closer to his children. This had meant giving up her job and moving away from her friends. The couple were struggling financially while Rhona looked for a job, which meant that travelling to see her old friends was also difficult. She felt that even if she did see them they didn't really understand how she felt or even how to help her. Rhona's partner was doing his best to help but was frustrated by her seeming lack of enthusiasm for their new life together.

The combination of moving house or location and having less in common with old friends, often means that stepparents become isolated, both physically and emotionally, from their friends. In addition to support from friends, support from family members is also often reduced for stepfamilies. When a couple separate or divorce, family members often experience divided loyalties. Typically, families remain loyal to biological members, however this is often complicated with grandparents and their grandchildren. While there is no biological tie between paternal grandparents and the biological mother, grandparents often feel compelled to remain loyal to their daughter-in-law in order to maintain strong links with their grandchildren. This can make it very difficult for their son's new partner. Stepmothers often find that they have a weaker relationship with their in-laws, which 'competes' with the existing relationship with the biological mother. This can increase the feelings of isolation for the stepmother and reduce the support provided, particularly in the early stages of the relationship.

Anna had been a stepmother for several years when I saw her. She had no children of her own but had a 10-year-old stepdaughter. Anna also had two nieces via her brother, who she was very close to. She struggled however with the inequality of the relationships that she and her brother had with the children. While she was very fond of her nieces, choosing birthday and Christmas presents for them, her brother didn't even acknowledge her stepdaughter, never buying cards or presents. This frustrated Anna as she felt he had simply not accepted his 'stepniece'. It also made her feel sad for her step-daughter, whom she felt was being treated poorly by her extended family. However when I asked Anna if she had ever talked to her brother about this she told me she hadn't but had just assumed his behaviour was because he didn't recognise her stepdaughter as part of her family. I encouraged Anna to talk to her brother, as this issue had created a rift in their relationship. It transpired that Anna's brother had not realised how his behaviour had affected his sister and was only too happy to make amends. Their relationship has now improved and the families spend more time together, which Anna is delighted with.

Practitioners should be cognisant of this dynamic and explore extended family relationships. It's vital that the couple is surrounded by as much support from family and friends as possible, particularly when they are in the early stages of the family development.

Differences between children in biological and stepfamilies

One of the hardest things for children in stepfamilies to adjust to is the sharing of time between their biological parents. If they still see both parents, children will spend time at two homes, possibly with distinctly different rules and expectations. They are also likely to face loyalty conflicts between their parents, with parents often fanning these flames, whether deliberately or accidentally. Children can often feel disloyal to one parent when they are enjoying time with the other, or even worry about leaving a parent on their own. Children are frequently put in difficult situations when moving between homes, often due to ongoing conflict between their parents.

When working with the adults, practitioners need to emphasise the importance of not involving children in ongoing disputes or conflict between the adults. As long as there is no threat to the child, either physically or mentally, the child should spend time with both parents and should be supported in these relationships. It is also important to give the children time to adjust when they arrive at a home, and to avoid 'quizzing' them about their time with the other parent. Let them talk in their own time and share things they are comfortable in sharing.

One of the most difficult aspects of parenting in stepfamilies is dealing with discipline. In biological families, both parents share in the disciplining of their children. While they have different views, the children accept that both parents have equal rights. In stepfamilies, the biological parent and stepparent start on an unequal footing. It's extremely difficult for a stepparent to discipline their stepchildren in the early stages of their relationship and it is therefore generally accepted, and supported by research, that stepparents should defer discipline issues to the biological parent in the early stages of their relationship. Over time, however, it's important for the stepparent to be able to enforce the rules of the household, with full support from the biological parent. Frequently, the stepparent can shy away from disciplining their stepchildren and instead, use the biological parent as the conduit: 'Please tell your son not to leave his dirty clothes on the floor.' This places the biological parent in a difficult position, where they can feel they are constantly giving 'bad news'. They can feel conflicting loyalty binds to their children and to their partner, with little room to please everyone!

In order to minimise this dynamic, practitioners should encourage a more balanced approach to discipline within the family. The couple need to have clear, unambiguous rules, which the children are aware of – for example, bedtime, use of mobile phones, language, manners – and which both adults enforce consistently. The children need to know that both adults apply the rules fairly and consistently. It's also important, particularly in the early stages of the relationship, that the biological parent doesn't undermine the stepparent in any decisions they've made with discipline.

Differences in family dynamics between biological and stepfamilies

Family membership in biological families is usually unambiguous. If you ask a member of a biological family to name the members of their own family, the responses tend to be fairly straightforward. However, ask the same question of stepfamilies and the answers are likely to be varied. Family Boundary Ambiguity is well documented, and relates to the lack of clarity as to who is included and who is excluded from the family (Boss and Greenberg, 1984). It is expected to be high among stepfamilies (Boss, 1980a), and refers to a 'state when family members are uncertain in their perception of who is in or out of the family or who is performing what roles or tasks within the family system' (Boss, 1987, p.709). It has also been suggested that boundaries have both physical and psychological dimensions, which foster a sense of identity that differentiates the members of a group from one another and from other groups (Boss, 1980b, 1987). This ambiguity is also related to increased family stress and overall family dysfunction (Minuchin, 1974; Boss and Greenberg, 1984; Boss, 1987).

However, it is recognised that ambiguous boundaries in stepfamilies result from the need for boundaries to have more flexibility as well as the need to redefine membership. There is also a difference in ambiguity between stepfamily types, with non-residential stepfamilies and more structurally complex stepfamilies experiencing more ambiguity (Pasley and Ihinger-Tallman, 1989; Stewart, 2005). Couples who have their own biological child in the new stepfamily often report lower ambiguity, so it appears that the birth of a child in some way encourages family integration (White and Booth, 1985; Bernstein, 1989, cited in Stewart, 2005; Beer, 1992, cited in Nielsen, 1999).

Our understanding of possible increased ambiguity in stepfamilies leads us to suggest that, in order to help stepfamilies develop and integrate, we need to help them find consensus about family membership. It is therefore important that practitioners work with families to identify any ambiguity related to family membership and help the family find a level of agreement.

Toolkit 1.1 My family

An exercise designed to help identify family ambiguity is provided at the end of the chapter. It is designed to be given to couples to identify differences in their perceptions of 'family' and to help provide early focus to therapeutic sessions.

Conclusion and key learning points

Stepfamilies are now recognised as the fastest-growing family type, not just in the UK but more broadly across the Western world. However, reliable statistics are difficult to find and generally capture only residential family units, ignoring families who may look after children only part-time. The stigma attached to the term 'stepfamily' also appears to affect individuals' desire to identify with being part of a stepfamily.

Some argue that it is irrelevant that we recognise the status of stepfamilies, and rather that they should be treated no differently to biological families. However there are a number of recognised differences between the two family types that can impact on the development and integration of the stepfamily. These differences can be divided into three distinct components:

1. Differences in the couple relationship
2. Differences that are felt by the children in the family
3. Differences for the wider family members.

The new couple have to manage a number of complex relationships and negotiate their own roles in the new family. They are also less likely to be surrounded by a good support network from family and friends, with wider family members feeling conflicting loyalty for biological and stepparents.

Children in stepfamilies are also likely to be affected by loyalty conflicts. Their loyalty to the biological parent can make it extremely difficult for them to form close bonds with their stepparent, which in turn can impact on the ability of the stepparent to integrate into the new family. Discipline is also a major flash-point in many stepfamilies. The advice is generally for stepparents to take a step back from disciplining their stepchildren in the early days of the relationship. However, this can be a very contentious issue for new couples as they clash over defining and implementing household rules regarding behaviour.

Finally, there are a number of differences between biological and stepfamilies that affect the wider family unit. It is recognised that stepfamilies take some time to integrate and develop. While the family forms instantly, the relationships take time to develop and grow. The new family has no history or traditions and these need to evolve over time. The membership of the new stepfamily is also ambiguous, with some members moving between households.

Toolkit

1.1 My family

This exercise can be used with couples to help identify ambiguity of family membership. It is useful for both the practitioner and the couple. Often each adult will include different individuals in their family and these differences will come as a surprise to their partners, leading to further discussion and debate. It's important to remember that there is no right or wrong answer – the difficulty occurs when the couple disagree over who is part of their family. It is important not to give specific guidance as they complete the form; individuals will invariably ask what is meant by 'family'. It's far better to let them interpret the phrase in their own way, as this is essential to the exercise. Some individuals only include biological relations, for example, while others include extended family members or even family pets! The main aim of the exercise is to identify similarity and areas of differences between the family members. This can then be used as a basis for further discussion in the counselling session.

List who is in your family and something you like doing with each one you have listed

Name	Activity

2 DEFINING STEPFAMILY TYPES

We tend to refer to stepfamilies as though they are a homogenous group. In reality there are many different types of stepfamily, each with its own challenges and stresses. This chapter will introduce the common types of stepfamily, based on the residency of the children and the family complexity. It will then explore the recognised issues that stepfamilies are known to experience. The key questions being addressed in this chapter are therefore as follows.

- What are the different types of stepfamily?
- What are the common problems faced by each stepfamily type?

Different types of stepfamily

Stepfamilies come in all shapes and sizes. The composition of the step-family often affects the issues they face, so it is vital to consider the family type when working with stepfamilies.

The key variables to consider are those based on family complexity and the residency of the children. Family complexity relates to whether one or both adults have children from prior relationships. If only one adult has prior children, then the family type is referred to as 'simple'. If both adults bring children from prior relationships the family type is referred to as 'complex'. In terms of residency, this relates to whether the children reside in the household or visit on a part-time basis. As such the families are referred to as 'full-time' or 'part-time'. An additional layer of family complexity is added when the step couple have further biological children together. While it could be argued that there is a full spectrum of residency options, with some children spending their entire time with one parent, through to children visiting a parent occasionally, the majority of literature differentiates purely on where the children reside from a legal perspective. This becomes their 'full-time' home and the other parent is considered 'part-time'. This book therefore considers four different types of stepfamily: simple part-time, complex part-time, simple full-time and complex full-time. More detailed definitions are provided below.

Simple part-time stepfamilies

This category describes stepfamilies where only one of the adults has children from a previous relationship and the children reside within the family on only a part-time basis.

> **Helen and Alex** had met at work two years ago. Helen had no children but Alex had three young children from a prior relationship. While the children lived predominantly with their mother they visited their father and Helen every other weekend. Helen and Alex are an example of a simple part-time stepfamily.

Stepparents in these stepfamilies may find it more difficult to fit in to their new family. They can also feel resentful of their stepchildren for the impact they've had on their lives. They are often confused about their role, which can in turn lead to them feeling anxious about their responsibilities.

Tips for part-time simple stepparents

- Always include your stepchildren in your definition of your family.
- Don't be afraid to ask for help if you're unsure what to do or how to act with your stepchildren. Talk to your partner.
- Keep expectations realistic – you are not going to become an instant parent.
- Learn to like your stepchildren and get to know them better.

- Try not to feel apprehensive or negative about your contact time. Be clear with your partner that you want to help them look after their children and want to be part of the fun, but you also need time out. In this way you are less likely to feel as resentful of the children's visits.

Simple full-time stepfamilies

This category describes stepfamilies where only one of the adults has children from a previous relationship. The stepchildren reside permanently within the family.

Clare and Steve have been together for three years. Clare has two children from her first marriage who live with her and Steve. They do still see their father regularly, though, and visit him at weekends and on one evening during the week. Clare and Steve are an example of a simple full-time stepfamily.

As one might expect, this type of stepparent tends to feel part of the new family relatively quickly as they are together as a family unit for the majority of the time. However they sometimes suffer from greater feelings of resentment towards their role, and often believe that they have less support from family and friends. Stepparents in this type of stepfamily take on the parenting role to their stepchildren full-time before they have their own biological children. This is a huge responsibility and has been shown to lead to resentment caused by the additional parenting demands.

Tips for full-time simple stepparents

- Make sure you make time for you and your partner.
- Don't lose contact with your old friends – and make time to catch up regularly.

- Get as much support as possible from grandparents or other relatives. It's all too easy to get dragged down with the stresses of family life and not make time for anything else.
- Don't bottle up your feelings. If you are frustrated then talk to your partner – or a friend if you find it easier. But, above all, avoid letting resentment build up and don't be afraid to accept all the help on offer.

Complex part-time stepfamilies

This category describes stepfamilies where both adults have children from previous relationships but the children reside with them on only a part-time basis, sharing their time between both biological parents.

Jane and Mike have been married for five years. Jane has two children who live with her for the majority of time but also visit their father regularly. Mike has a teenage son who lives with his mother but spends a lot of time with Jane and Mike. They are an example of a complex part-time stepfamily as not all the children reside in the household.

As these stepparents already have children of their own, the move to the new stepfamily is not such a big change and they tend to cope better with the transition, often with more confidence and less anxiety about how to deal with their stepchildren. However, they tend to find it more difficult to bond with their stepchildren than do the full-time stepparents. This is related to feelings of jealousy and an inherent bond with their biological children. Stepparents in this position can find it hard to balance the demands of their stepchildren and their biological children.

Tips for part-time complex stepparents

- Accept that it will take time to develop a close relationship with your stepchildren. Be patient.

- Let your affection for your stepchildren develop slowly and naturally – don't force the pace.
- Remember to include everyone in your family – including part-time members!
- Adopt a more flexible approach to parenting.

Complex full-time stepfamilies

This category describes stepfamilies where both adults have children from previous relationships and one or all of the children live permanently with the couple.

Alison and Bill *have been together for the past seven years. Bill is a widower with two teenage children. Alison has a daughter from a previous relationship who lives with Alison and Bill. She does still see her father but not very often as he lives in another part of the country. Alison and Bill are an example of a complex full-time stepfamily as the children all live with them for the majority of the time.*

Individuals who are stepparents in this type of family often find it easier to truly feel part of the stepfamily as they take on a much more traditional parenting role to their stepchildren. These stepparents have a great deal of parenting responsibility. In addition to their own children, they are caring for their stepchildren full-time, which in turn increases demands on them – physically, emotionally and financially. This type of stepparent must find a way to maintain a balance between the demands on their time, finances and emotions.

Tips for full-time complex stepparents
- Make time for yourself – whether it's coffee with friends or a night at the pictures with your partner.
- If your stepchildren are old enough, make sure they help around the house where possible.

> ● If your stepchildren are younger, call on friends or neighbours to help with babysitting. You could even set up a babysitting circle, where you can trade favours with your friends.

Figure 2.1 illustrates the key family types.

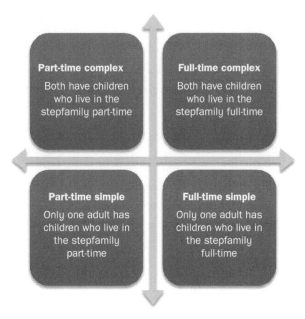

Part-time complex
Both have children who live in the stepfamily part-time

Full-time complex
Both have children who live in the stepfamily full-time

Part-time simple
Only one adult has children who live in the stepfamily part-time

Full-time simple
Only one adult has children who live in the stepfamily full-time

Figure 2.1 The four common stepfamily types

Different types – different issues

While some of the stresses of stepfamily life are universal, many of them vary depending on the complexity of the family and the residency of the children. A number of researchers have addressed the issue of differences within stepfamily structures by identifying differences between complex and simple stepfamilies (e.g. Schultz, Schultz and Olson, 1991; Ganong *et al.*, 1999; O'Connor and Insabella, 1999; Johnson *et al.*, 2008).

Complex stepfamilies, for example, have been found to experience lower marital satisfaction and higher stress than simple stepfamilies (Clingempeel and Brand, 1985; Schultz *et al.*, 1991). Role ambiguity has also been found to be higher in complex stepfamilies (Fine and Schwebel, 1991; Stewart, 2005), with researchers suggesting that the heightened role ambiguity is due to the fact that both parents in the stepfamily are simultaneously biological parents *and* stepparents. White (1998) found evidence of this heightened ambiguity in complex stepfamilies, with the adults frequently disagreeing on the number of children that should be considered part of the family unit.

Despite evidence suggesting that complex stepfamilies suffer from more difficulties in the remarriage than simple stepfamilies, a limited amount of research has suggested the opposite. Brown (1987) found that complex stepfamilies had less difficulty in adapting to life in the stepfamily than those in other types of stepfamily, with the role becoming easier over time. Brown suggested that this might be due to the fact that, as each adult is both a stepparent and a biological parent, they can more fully empathise and understand the conflicting demands experienced by their partners.

Turning to the residency of stepchildren, research has for example suggested that non-residential stepparenting is more stressful and less rewarding for women than residential stepparenting (Ambert, 1986). In addition, families with non-residential stepchildren have been found to suffer heightened boundary ambiguity (Stewart, 2005), with a lack of clarity over membership of the family.

The following section explores some of the issues stepfamilies experience and identifies differences based on family type.

Mental wellbeing

There is significant consensus between stepfamily researchers and clinicians that there is a high level of stress involved in being a stepparent (Burgoyne and Clark, 1984, cited in Church, 1999; Pasley and Ihinger-Tallman, 1988; Hetherington, 1993) and that the stresses are greater for stepmothers than stepfathers (Furstenberg and Nord, 1985; Morrison and Thompson-Guppy, 1985; Ahrons and Wallisch, 1987; MacDonald and DeMaris, 1996).

As early as the 1940s, researchers were investigating the effects of stress in stepfamilies on the mental health wellbeing of stepmothers. Researchers have consistently found that stepmothers have significantly higher anxiety than biological mothers, at levels likely to affect their ability to cope effectively (Pfleger, 1947, and Nadler, 1977, both cited in Morrison and Thompson-Guppy, 1985). A further study found the majority of stepmothers were experiencing identity confusion mixed with feelings of helplessness and ineffectiveness. They reported feeling exhausted under the pressures and expectations of the family situation (Morrison and Thompson-Guppy, 1985). Further research has found evidence to suggest that stepmothers in complex stepfamilies have significantly greater feelings of depression than women in other family types (Clingempeel *et al.*, 1985; Schultz *et al.*, 1991; O'Connor and Insabella, 1999), suggesting that these individuals struggle to cope with the added complexities that their family type demands.

The effects on mental health have been shown to affect not just the adults within the stepfamilies but also the children. A study by Barrett and Turner (2005), to investigate whether family type is associated with differences in mental health problems, found significantly lower levels of depressive symptoms among young adults from biological families compared to other family norms including stepfamilies and single-parent families. The children from stepfamilies were found to report more stressful life events and less supportive family relationships than those from biological families. These findings suggest that individuals' mental health wellbeing, regardless of family structure, is protected by strong family support. There is further evidence to suggest that non-residential stepparenting is more stressful and less rewarding than residential stepparenting (Ambert, 1986), with non-residential stepfamilies additionally suffering heightened boundary ambiguity (Stewart, 2005).

Overall, these findings suggest that the mental health wellbeing of individuals is negatively affected by stepfamily life, with factors including social support, an increase in life events and socioeconomic status mediating their perceived depression and anxiety (O'Connor *et al.*, 1998; Barrett and Turner, 2005).

Undefined roles for stepparents

The issue of role clarity is a well-recognised and researched issue within stepfamilies (e.g. Orchard and Solberg, 1999; Weaver and Coleman, 2005), with research suggesting that the stepparent often lacks a role model and whatever expectations they have tend to be unrealistic. As a consequence some stepparents feel frustrated in trying to fill a largely undefined role for which they have no training. Fine (1995) suggests that, given the relative infrequency of stepmothers residing with their stepchildren, it can be argued that they have fewer socially accepted role prescriptions than stepfathers, leading to greater role ambiguity.

> **Toolkit 2.1 Defining the stepparents' role in the family**
>
> *An exercise to help stepparents understand their role in the new family unit is provided at the end of the chapter.*

Conflicting parental roles

Role theory (MacDonald and DeMaris, 1996) suggests that everyday life is based around living up to expectations of different roles, with individuals assuming many different roles depending on their social circumstances. When applied to stepfamily dynamics, individuals assume multiple roles such as stepmother and biological mother or stepfather and biological father. Role theory has been used to suggest that it is the resultant conflict between these roles within stepfamilies that causes increased stress. Visher and Visher (1979) suggested that, when stepmothers have biological children for the first time, they experience intense role conflict as they try to assume both the stepmother and biological mother role simultaneously. A later study, by McDonald and DeMaris (1996), found that this conflict was evident in both stepmothers and stepfathers. Research into the issues faced by stepparents (Beaudry *et al.*, 2001) has suggested that the difficulties within stepfamilies revolve around the roles of the spouse, the parent and the stepparent impacting on the marital satisfaction within the relationship. The use of role theory to explain stepfamily behaviour has not been widely used (Stewart, 2007), however it could potentially be used to explain differences between different types of stepfamily based on their complexity. Role theory suggests that, the more roles an individual is expected to play, the more conflict they are likely to experience. Consequently, according to this theory, stepfamilies with more complex households would suffer the most stress.

Couple relationship

Marital satisfaction is one of the most widely studied variables across family research, yet also one of the most confusing in terms of clear findings (Vemer *et al.*, 1989). Family researchers have historically considered the married couple relationship to be the most important relationship in the family (Minuchin, 1974; Belsky, 1984), with a good marriage providing a supportive framework to the family unit. A high proportion of the research into marital satisfaction has focused on remarriages, in an effort to understand where differences may lie between first and subsequent marriages, and identifying the issues within remarriages (White and Booth, 1985; Hobart, 1991; O'Connor and Insabella, 1999).

A number of studies (White and Booth, 1985; Hobart, 1991; O'Connor and Insabella, 1999) have drawn comparisons between first marriages and remarriages, with the inherent assumption that first marriages provide the norm against which to measure marital satisfaction. A meta-analysis on remarital satisfaction found evidence from 16 studies to suggest that people in first marriages report greater satisfaction than those in remarriages, however the differences were small and not significant (Vemer *et al.*, 1989). A longitudinal study of divorced, remarried and non-divorced families, conducted by Hetherington (1993), found that, in the first two years of a remarriage, remarried couples reported higher marital satisfaction than longer married, never divorced couples. However, over time, no differences in marital satisfaction were found.

However, the presence of stepchildren in the remarried household, and problems associated with the relationships between stepparent and stepchildren, appear to affect the stability of second marriages. For example, White and Booth (1985) found the presence of stepchildren was related to an increase in marriage breakdown rates, whereas for couples with no stepchildren in the household, marriage breakdown rates did not differ from first-marriage breakdown rates. Thus it is possible that the high dissolution rate of second marriages is caused by conflict between family members rather than marital distress per se (Lawton and Sanders, 1994). It has been suggested that children in the remarriage may make it more difficult for the couple to find enough time to solidify their relationship and so strengthen the marital bond (Pill, 1990). There is also some evidence that there are more difficulties in the couple relationship related to biological children brought in to the stepfamily from the father than the mother (Hobart, 1991; Knox and Zusman, 2001).

A difference between stepfamilies based on their complexity has also been found related to their marital happiness, with a higher remarriage divorce rate limited to complex stepfamilies (White and Booth, 1985) and greater perceived happiness in the relationship for simple stepfamilies (Clingempeel, 1981).

Toolkit 2.2 Our great relationship

An exercise to help couples improve their relationship is provided at the end of the chapter.

Age and sex of stepchildren

Research has shown that the age of children when entering the stepfamily can have a significant effect on the overall success of the family unit (Hetherington, Cox and Cox, 1982; Fine, Coleman and Ganong, 1998; Marsiglio, 2004). It can also have an impact on the development of the stepparent–stepchild relationship and the potential for bonding. When children are less than 9 years of age there is a greater likelihood of acceptance of the stepchild by the stepparent and acceptance of the stepparent as a parent by the stepchild (Hetherington *et al.*, 1982; Fine *et al.*, 1998; Marsiglio, 2004). There is some limited evidence that stepparent–stepdaughter relationships in both stepmother and stepfather families are more problematic than stepparent–stepson relationships (Clingempeel, Brand and Ievoli, 1984).

Mutual children

A limited amount of research has been conducted over the years to investigate the effects of a child born into a stepfamily. Ganong and Coleman (1988) conducted a study to investigate whether a mutual baby strengthened emotional ties in the new relationship. They found no difference between stepfamilies who had had joint children and those who hadn't. Moreover, evidence from other studies has suggested that a mutual child can have a disruptive impact on step relationships (Visher and Visher, 1979; Berman, 1980, cited in Ganong and Coleman, 1988). A more recent study, by Stewart (2005), reported that the addition of a half sibling is not beneficial to stepchildren and that childbearing lessens involvement with existing children. In a study directed at understanding parenting aspects of both biological and stepchildren, MacDonald and DeMaris (1996) found evidence to suggest that, if the mutual child is the first biological child born to either the stepfather or stepmother, they will struggle to appreciate or enjoy the company of their stepchildren, however they found no evidence to indicate that the birth of a mutual biological child had an effect on stepparents' perception of difficulty in rearing their stepchildren. The findings also suggested that the addition of a mutual child leads to more role conflict for the spouse who has just become a biological parent, as they struggle to cope with the combined stepparent and biological parent roles. In addition, stepfathers have also been shown to experience cognitive dissonance with respect to resources for all the children following the birth of a biological child (Clingempeel, Colyar and Hetherington, 1994; MacDonald and DeMaris, 1996).

In conclusion, research conducted to determine the effect of the birth of a mutual child, suggests a largely negative (e.g. Visher and Visher, 1979; Berman, 1980, cited in Ganong and Coleman, 1988; MacDonald and DeMaris, 1996) or at best neutral impact (Ganong *et al.*, 1988; Stewart, 2005) on the wellbeing of the stepfamily.

Conclusion and key learning points

This chapter has sought to explore the different types of stepfamily, considering both family complexity and the residency of the children. Research has identified a number of consistent and unique differences that in turn affect the family's functioning. There are also significant differences based on the gender of the stepparent, with stepmothers and stepfathers experiencing different types of stressors and demands.

Finally, the chapter has introduced and discussed many of the common issues that are known to affect stepfamilies, together with the differences based on family type. Research has suggested that stepmothers experience greater anxiety than biological mothers and this can differ significantly depending on the complexity and residency of the children. Similarly, role ambiguity is a problem shared by a great number of stepparents and this, too, varies depending on stepfamily type. Practitioners should perhaps also pay close attention to the ages and sex of children within the family as evidence has suggested that these can play a significant part in the integration of the new family unit.

Toolkit

2.1 Defining the stepparents' role in the family

The following questions are useful for professionals to use to help stepparents understand their current role in the stepfamily. It may be that this needs to be clarified or even changed, however it is important that both adults agree on the boundaries of roles.

- Ask the stepparent(s) to think about their current role in the stepfamily.
- How would they describe it? What words best encompass the role: friend, parent?
- What activities do they do regularly *with* their stepchild(ren)?
- What things do they do *for* their stepchild(ren)?
- Do they get involved in disciplining their stepchild(ren)?
- Do they share the parenting of the children in the house with their partner?
- Are they happy with their current role?
- If not, how would they like it to change and what needs to happen?

2.2 Our great relationship: an exercise for couples

This exercise is a powerful promoter of a good marriage or partnership. When used regularly it improves teamwork and the feeling that both partners want the relationship to succeed. The trick is to make a regular commitment to carrying it out at a time that suits both individuals. Give a copy of the form on the next page to them and suggest they photocopy it a few times and fill it in. Encourage them to stick the results on their fridge to remind themselves of their goals.

Our great relationship

Take it in turns to choose one topic per session. The only rule is that you don't blame or get negative, but listen carefully to what your partner is saying and don't interrupt them. After 5 minutes (or 10) you should swap listening for talking. The main benefit is in listening to your partner, rather than trying to solve the problem. Be disciplined and finish on time.

1. Where will we hold our regular talking and listening sessions? i.e. garden, sitting room ....
2. How many times per week (e.g. once, twice?) and which days/ times ....
3. How long will we each speak for? (5 minutes, 10 minutes each, etc.) ....
4. How will we avoid a row or blaming? ....
5. What will we discuss? Choose one topic per session from the following or add a topic.

My children

Your children

Our children

My ex

Your ex

How I'd like our social life to be

How do we discipline our children?

Something else to do with friends/family

Spending time

How we spend our time, apart and together

What I'd like to be different

Your interests/hobbies

My interests/hobbies

Something else to do with our time

Worries

I'm worried about …

What worries you?

How can we help each other when we feel down?

Something else about worries

Feeling

How I want to feel loved in our stepfamily; how I feel now

How I want to feel

What I love about you

What I'd like to be different in our relationship

Sex

How I show I love you

How you show you love me

What I'd like for our intimate relationship

Something else about sex

Home

What I like about our home

What I'd like to be different

Sharing chores

Something else about home

Life/future

What I want from life

My hopes for the future

Your hopes for the future

How can we grow as a couple?

My fears

Something else about the future

3 INTRODUCING INTEGRATED STEPFAMILY THERAPY (IST)

This chapter sets out a new model for providing tailored support, specifically targeted at stepfamilies. The approach presented here is theoretically sound, based on empirical evidence from research and existing theories. However, it is also practical, offering a repeatable, easy to follow set of guidelines for professionals working with stepfamilies. This chapter will address the following questions.

- Why is a distinctive approach to counselling needed for stepfamilies?
- What are the goals of Integrated Stepfamily Therapy?
- What are the strengths of existing models of stepfamily therapy, and how have these informed Integrated Stepfamily Therapy?

A new approach to stepfamily counselling

The therapist didn't seem to understand us at all. She said that we must have known what we were heading into when we decided to live together.

(**Jo**, biological and stepmum)

We contacted our local council to ask if they could offer us any support as a new stepfamily. They suggested we sign up for a parenting course they were running. Unfortunately this just made us feel worse! We felt excluded and isolated from the other couples that were not from stepfamilies and the advice given assumed that the children lived with us all the time. It was so frustrating.

(**John and Maddie**, stepdad and biological mum)

These quotes were all taken from couples I've seen over the past few years. Clearly, many stepfamilies do find support when they need help with stepfamily-related issues, however we shouldn't ignore the fact that many stepfamilies struggle to find the help they need from relationship experts.

The second quote, from **Maddie**, shows that sometimes offering the same support for stepfamilies can actually make things worse, serving only to highlight the differences between biological and stepfamilies, and the inherent difficulties stepfamilies face. I argue that, *to be effective, counselling offered to stepfamilies should be targeted and focused.* The family should not be compared to 'normal' biological families or offered interventions that were primarily designed for first families. There are too many differences between the family types that make these interventions difficult to apply consistently and effectively in stepfamilies.

Integrated Stepfamily Therapy (IST) adopts a behavioural, solutions-focused rather than a therapeutic approach. Practitioners who are familiar with **Solution Focused Brief Therapy (SFBT)** may draw parallels between the two approaches to couple therapy, and indeed there are similarities. SFBT is a therapy based on social constructionist philosophy. It was developed by de Shazer and Berg in the late 1970s and, as the name suggests, is *future focused, goal directed* and *focused on solutions* rather than problems. However, a distinct difference between the two approaches is in the role of the therapist. SFBT specifically aims to 'leave no footprints in [its] clients' lives' (de Jong and Berg, 1998), whereas the approach recommended for practitioners working with stepfamilies is to work with them to identify solutions, sometimes taking the lead to identify potential compromises or alternative ways forward when the couples become entrenched in their views. Despite these differences, it's worth looking at some of the key assumptions of SFBT (Ratner, George and Iveson, 2012), as I believe these are all equally applicable (see Table 3.1).

The aim of the approach is therefore to help stepfamilies understand the development process of their new family unit and learn ways of tolerating differences between biological and stepfamilies. They need to learn to accept their unique family structure before moving on to address the challenges. The focus is therefore on making small, manageable changes in their beliefs and behaviours, and is based primarily on interventions for the couple, rather than between other family members. In making these changes, the couple are able to trigger significant

Table 3.1   Key interventions for IST

SFBT assumption	IST approach
Some changes may already have happened but these have gone unnoticed by the client	Here it's important to talk to the client about what's going well in their couple relationship and stepfamily – as well as what isn't going so well. Often individuals focus on the problems rather than recognising successes. I usually find that clients focus on the negative and fail to notice often significant successes in the development of their families. Given that change happens slowly, and stepfamily relationships develop and strengthen over months and years, it is often useful to remind the client of these changes so that they have a much more balanced perspective and realistic view
Each session can be treated as though it may be the last	The sessions should be self-contained and focused on addressing particular issues within the stepfamily. The aim is to leave the session with specific, focused advice that the family can try to use to effect positive changes. Often the clients need only a minimal number of sessions to feel more confident and able to tackle the issues independently
Change in one element of a system will effect other elements, therefore only a small change may be necessary to initiate further change in a system (de Shazer, 1985)	A stepfamily comprises a number of subsystems (e.g. the stepparent–stepchild, the biological parent–stepparent, the biological parent–ex partner). Effecting a change in one of these subsystems can have a ripple-through effect in other relationships. For example, if the stepparent and the biological parent can develop a shared view of discipline, the relationship between stepparent and stepchildren is likely to be improved, due to the increased clarity of the stepparenting role
Solution-focused work tends to have longer intervals between sessions, allowing clients more time to implement changes. So four sessions may well extend over a 10- or 12-week period, depending on the needs of the client	The aim of solution-focused work is to identify some potential changes in behaviour for the individuals within the stepfamily. Therefore it's important to give the family enough time to implement the changes and identify any positive outcomes or further issues. Scheduling sessions too close together means that there isn't sufficient time to notice any changes

(continued)

Table 3.1   Key interventions for IST (*continued*)

SFBT assumption	IST approach
Practitioners tend to believe that most clients have better ways to spend their time than talking to therapists, and therefore think of therapy as short interventions in people's lives, enabling them to move on with their lives	This brief approach to stepfamily therapy is welcomed by clients, many of whom have never been to a therapist or counsellor before. Often they are overwhelmed by the problems they are facing in their family, but struggle with the concept of therapy. The brief therapy approach offers them flexible access to support, which they can turn to whenever they feel they are struggling. This approach was also described in the model of Brief Therapy developed by Burt and Burt (1996) in their work with stepfamilies (discussed later in this chapter)

changes that ripple through their extended support structure, including extended family and friends.

The development of any theoretical model should be clearly dependent on underpinning theory and research. This model is no exception; it has been developed using international peer-reviewed research and builds on earlier models of stepfamily development from eminent researchers and clinicians, including Visher and Visher (1996), Papernow (1993, 2013), and Burt and Burt (1996). These models are described and critiqued in the following sections.

Visher model

This approach relied on evidence from a study investigating the experiences of stepfamily couples in therapy (Pasley *et al.*, 1996). The study involved 267 couples and explored their experiences of therapy. Four specific interventions were identified as being particularly useful for stepfamilies:

1. validating and normalising stepfamily dynamics – helping clients understand that initial difficulties are normal and to be expected
2. supplying important psycho-education – to communicate the common issues stepfamilies face and to provide them with more realistic expectations
3. reducing helplessness – helping clients to focus on what is within their control and to let go of things outside their control
4. building the couple relationship – the couple is the foundation of the new stepfamily – without it the family does not exist; the couple need help in strengthening and building their partnership.

In addition to these four key areas, the Vishers identified a number of secondary interventions, which they believed should also be included in therapy with stepfamilies. These are as follows.

- Assisting with recognition and acceptance of losses – helping the clients understand that, with change, comes inevitable losses. This may be in terms of moving house, changing jobs or, for children, it may mean having to share a bedroom, a change in the sibling order in the household, or even the new rules and roles in the family.
- Sharing past histories and forming new rituals and memories – helping couples understand that past experiences can impact on their present relationship and encouraging them to create their own shared memories, taking the best from previous relationships and building their own shared ideas.
- Identifying potential solutions – stepfamilies seek therapy at a time when there is considerable stress in their family. They are often experiencing increased anxiety and depression, and hence are unable to work through the issues logically and rationally. The therapist is ideally placed to identify potential solutions and discuss these with the couple.
- Separate feelings from behaviour – while stepparents may not have the same feelings for their stepchildren as their own biological children, it is vital that they behave in the same way to all the children, regardless of their relationship.
- Teaching negotiation – building common rules that all the family can abide by and live with. This may well involve negotiation and compromise.
- Restructure and reframe – helping the couple to interpret behaviour in the context of change and loss. For example, if a child is clinging to a biological parent it should not be interpreted that they don't like their stepparent, just recognised that they are coming to terms with change and loss.
- Use accurate language – many stepfamilies avoid the 'step' label. It is important to recognise when this is happening and use clear terms that reflect reality rather than reinforce unrealistic expectations. Ensure children understand that stepparents are not replacing parents.

If couples are given support in these areas, they are more likely to be able to cope more effectively with the challenges they are facing and move on with the development of their family unit. Worryingly, more than half of the respondents in the original study mentioned that there were aspects of the therapy they had found unhelpful. Several had seen a number of therapists before finding one who was helpful to them.

> The therapist expected us to feel and act like a nuclear family, and that's a lie.

> We saw three therapists in five years before we got to one who knew anything at all about stepfamilies. Our situation had continued to deteriorate and we couldn't understand what was wrong and why we couldn't be helped.

> The therapist believed I loved my stepchild and when I said I didn't – he couldn't quite get it.

> (Visher and Visher, 1996, p.12)

While this research took place some years ago, my own research, conducted in 2013, identified similar patterns, where couples had tried several therapists before finding one who they felt was truly able to understand the unique stepfamily issues. Clearly, if therapists are to provide the support needed by stepfamilies, they need to truly understand the differences and common challenges.

Papernow model

Papernow (1984, 1996) identified seven stages of normal stepfamily development, which follow one another chronologically. Progression from one stage to the next depends upon a degree of success in meeting the challenges of the previous stage. Families vary widely in the length of time they take to progress through the cycle, but Papernow (1984) points out that no family she studied took less than four years. Moreover, seven years was the average period of time for progression and some families remained trapped in the early stages after as long as 12 years, with divorce resulting in a number of families that had failed to progress. Papernow (1984, 1996) based her theoretical framework on interviews with 50 stepfamilies, many of whom were drawn from her own clinical practice.

Papernow also introduces the concept of the middle ground (Nevis and Watner, 1983) to identify the differences between stepfamilies and biological families. The middle ground refers to the areas of agreement in a relationship. Here the individuals will often agree on the way forward, with little need for discussion. Over time, the thickening of the middle ground makes living together easier as couples become more familiar with each other. When the middle ground is thin, however, there is little room for agreement and many areas that require resolution and compromise. When relating this theory to stepfamilies, it is clear to see that they start with thick middle ground in parent–child relationships and thin middle ground in the new adult step couple and stepparent–stepchild relationships. It is therefore these relationships that require attention, often calling for skills in listening and conflict resolution.

Building from these cornerstones and her extensive work in the field, Papernow developed a framework that she calls the stepfamily architecture (Papernow, cited in Pryor, 2008). This is based on five major challenges that she believes stepfamilies face:

1. insider/outsider roles – biological parents and children form close units, leaving the stepparent feeling excluded
2. children bring losses and loyalty binds, with children feeling torn both between biological parents and between biological and stepparents (i.e. If I like my stepmum, am I being disloyal to my mum?)
3. parents come to the new family with a strong emotional connection with their children, however stepparents have no such ties; consequently the stepparent often adopts a more authoritarian approach, whereas biological parents, particularly after experiencing relationship losses and change, are frequently more permissive
4. the new family needs to create its own identity from two disparate units
5. a recognition that stepfamily boundaries extend beyond the immediate family unit and include at least one parent who affects, and is affected by, what happens in the stepfamily.

In order to meet these challenges Papernow suggests a number of strategies, which therapists may wish to utilise with stepfamilies. These include:

- normalising the effects of stepfamily dynamics
- encouraging stepfamily members to spend time developing one-to-one relationships with other family members, so reducing the insider/outside issue and building the middle ground in the new relationships
- assisting the adults in understanding and in helping to reduce the children's loyalty binds
- setting realistic expectations of stepparents and stepchildren

- encouraging the stepparent to follow the lead of the parent in terms of parenting and discipline, particularly in the early stages of the family's development
- managing change to ensure it is steady and consistent – the development of the new family shouldn't be rushed
- encouraging the biological parent to aim to reduce conflict with the absent parent and finally to establish boundaries between the households – for example, limiting access to the new family home for the ex partner or perhaps agreeing to limit discussion between the biological parents to issues relating to care of the children.

A final aspect to Papernow's model is the concept of a three-level approach to the intervention – psycho-educational, interpersonal and intrapsychic – which she refers to as the 'what', 'how' and 'why' (Papernow, cited in Pryor, 2008).

The psycho-educational support helps stepfamily members to adopt more realistic expectations in terms of family development and relationships. However, while this may be a relief for some who realise that their experiences are normal and to be expected, for others it signifies an unexpected loss of aspirations and beliefs. Papernow (cited in Pryor, 2008) therefore suggests that therapists need to approach this stage with empathic connection, recognising the difficulties the stepfamily is experiencing.

Papernow (cited in Pryor, 2008) then emphasises the need to enhance communication skills within the stepfamily, recognising that in order to deal with the differences and demands of stepfamily architecture, individuals need to have mature communication skills. She recommends that therapists first try to understand how the couple communicate presently, identifying patterns and traits. For example, do they accuse (e.g. 'You never support me, you always side with your children') or attack (e.g. 'I can't believe you let them get away with that behaviour again'), or are they more collaborative (e.g. 'I wish I had more confidence in enforcing house rules. Will you help me?'). It's important to understand the current communication patterns before trying to instil new, more effective ones. Given that these skills are difficult to teach, Papernow (cited in Pryor, 2008) suggests that therapists should aim to focus on one or two new techniques. An example of this is the soft start-up (Gottman and Silver, 1999), which aims to introduce difficult topics by starting with positive intentions and expressing empathy.

For example, 'I know you don't want to feel you're always having to tell Mark off when he comes to stay, but I think its only reasonable that he tidies up his room. It's always such a mess when he leaves. Would you mind having a word with him?'

The third stage of Papernow's intervention (cited in Pryor, 2008) is related to understanding more about why particular issues or skills are hard for certain individuals. Papernow warns that therapists with experience in working with individual clients may be tempted to start therapy at this stage, however she suggests that in doing so they will fail to address more fundamental issues that are related purely to stepfamily dynamics and relationships. Often, by providing psycho-education and enhancing communication skills, they will be able to help clients resolve their problems and enable their family to continue developing. Papernow (cited in Pryor, 2008) suggests that prematurely engaging in intrapsychic-level work without meeting the basic needs for guidance and information is a mistake and does not effectively address the needs of stepfamilies.

Papernow's approach is therefore both recognition of the distinct differences and issues that often overwhelm stepfamilies, and a need to deal with issues layer by layer. The presenting issues may well be purely related to the demands of stepfamily life and can be addressed simply and effectively, without resorting to deeper intrapsychic work.

Burt and Burt: Step by Step model (1996)

The Burt and Burt Step by Step model is also based on the view that stepfamilies are structurally different from biological families and, as such, traditional models of therapy are ineffective. They argue that traditional therapies, such as intrapsychic and psychodynamic, do not focus on these specific needs and therefore don't address the needs of the stepfamily.

This model also focuses on the couple relationship, recognising its fragility and importance in the new family. In strengthening the couple bond, Burt and Burt argue that the benefits of the therapy will strengthen not only the couple, but all the relationships within it, as the changes ripple through the family. Their approach to therapy is through Brief Treatment, which they have developed over 15 years of working with stepfamilies. The Step by Step model is similar to other Brief Therapy models philosophically (e.g. Cummings, 1990), and argues that therapy should be accessed briefly, throughout an individual's life, and be used for focusing on crises generated by developmental changes. Therapy can therefore be seen as interrupted rather than terminated (Zeig and Gilligan, 1990). Prospective clients are told that the therapy is likely to be brief because of the ongoing development of the stepfamily and the evolving nature of the likely difficulties. They are therefore encouraged to return to the therapist when they are struggling with future changes and as difficulties present themselves.

Burt and Burt see the therapist in this model as a teacher and guide through family transitions, able to signpost clients to other services and support as required. The model is process oriented, assisting clients to seek solution-focused responses to problems. These solutions can include education, skill building (including problem solving, negotiation, compromise and communication), and the development of effective coping strategies and skills.

Their model is based on four assumptions, as follows.

1. Stepfamilies are 'normal' families. They should therefore not be treated as though they are 'abnormal', although they do differ from biological families.
2. The development processes drive the stepfamily adjustment, with many changes occurring over a protracted period of time. Education helps reduce the helplessness often felt by stepparents.
3. The structure of a stepfamily predicts issues that will be a focus of treatment.
4. Expectations and beliefs about stepfamilies need to be examined and made more realistic.

Given the flexibility of the model, there are only two real stages to the intervention: initial assessment and triage.

The assessment is devoted to understanding the family dynamics and identifying the main problems the couple want to address. The therapist needs to encourage controlled ventilation, obtain a genogram and develop an initial understanding of the family dynamics and relationships. The early client sessions are therefore focused on extracting key information from the couple, while providing education related to the four assumptions. Once this process is complete the therapist moves to the triage phase, which ensures that time and energy are channelled into areas that can realistically be changed through therapy. During this stage, the therapist works with the couple to strengthen their relationship, to identify workable issues, to organise overwhelming ones and to help the couple cope more effectively with the children.

Burt and Burt (1996) offer strategies to help focus these efforts. A good example of this is their use of Monopoly money. They suggest giving each adult some different denominations of Monopoly money and asking them to choose three problems they would like to focus on. By allocating different amounts of money to each, the client can indicate the priority of each of the problems to them – and the therapist can clearly see the differences in priorities between the couple.

Comparison of established models

The three models presented above all provide sound research-based approaches to improving outcomes for stepfamilies, and many of the planned interventions are common between them. In particular, the models all prioritise the four key areas described below.

Four key interventions to improving outcomes

1. *Normalise experiences*: to work with stepfamilies to validate that their experiences are normal and to be expected.
2. *Establish realistic expectations*: to challenge some of the more unrealistic expectations that stepfamily members may have adopted.
3. *Psycho-education*: to continue to provide psycho-education as part of the therapy, helping stepfamily members to understand the differences between the family types and to strengthen their ability to cope more effectively with the unique stepfamily issues.
4. *Strengthen couple bond*: continue building and supporting the couple relationship, which is the newest and most fragile within the new family unit. This involves helping the couple communicate effectively, improving listening and conflict resolution in the early stages.

My own research and work with stepfamilies resonates strongly with these priorities. Research on stepmothers in the UK (Doodson, 2014; Doodson and Davies, 2014) identified that they experience significantly increased anxiety over biological mothers. When questioned in focus groups, it became clear that the anxiety was primarily related to two areas, as described below.

Two types of anxiety

1. *Anxiety related to the stepparental role:* given that there are no clear guidelines or social norms for stepparents, individuals find it difficult to understand their role in the new family, particularly with respect to their stepchildren, leading to ambiguity, confusion and further stress.

2. *Anxiety related to the absent biological parent:* stepparents frequently feel they have little or no control within their family unit, caused by the influence of the absent biological parent. These issues in particular lead to greater feelings of helplessness. Research related to the relationship between control and mental health wellbeing suggests that, for new parents (biological and step), impairment in control is associated with depression, stress and anxiety-related disorders (Shapiro, Schwartz and Astin, 1996; Chorpita *et al.*, 1998; Mirowsky *et al.*, 1999; Keeton *et al.*, 2008). Stepparents are therefore vulnerable if they are forced to deal with significant continued involvement from the absent biological parent.

Both of these findings are addressed within the Papernow and Visher models. Papernow, for example, talks of the need to improve and clarify the boundary with the ex partner and the need for the parent to initially lead in areas of discipline. Visher, and Burt and Burt highlight the importance of reducing helplessness by increasing the sense of control within the stepfamily. If practitioners can focus on interventions aimed at reducing anxiety and depression they are likely to improve the overall mental wellbeing within the stepfamily.

Synthesising interventions from these recognised approaches and my own UK-based research suggests that, when working with stepfamilies, the following interventions are key:

- normalise the stepfamily experiences
- establish realistic expectations

- strengthen the couple bond and enhance communication
- help the couple define clear, unambiguous stepparent roles
- provide clear boundaries for communication with the ex partner.

I will now look at each of these in turn.

Normalise the stepfamily experiences

Many couples seeking help feel isolated and often ashamed of their feelings towards their stepchildren. While the number of stepfamilies is growing, it's often difficult for stepfamilies to meet other families in the same situation and thus validate their own feelings. It is therefore important that family professionals take the time to normalise the feelings and experiences of the couple. They need to reassure the couple that their experiences are normal and to be expected in developing and integrating their new family. One of the primary ways of achieving this is through explaining the 'stepfamily cycle' discussed earlier in the chapter. By helping couples understand the processes that are taking place in their family, they are able to relax and give each other time to adjust to the many changes. Only by taking this approach can the couple hope to move on to the next stage of their development. Stepparents are often overwhelmed by their feelings as they try to integrate their new families, however they find it extremely difficult to discuss these feelings with their partners for fear of upsetting them.

> *Nicola* *had been with her partner for three years and was finding it increasingly difficult to cope with weekends when her stepsons came to visit. She found that her partner's attitude to her daughter changed when his children came to visit. He spent more time with his sons and appeared to be lenient in his treatment of them. Her daughter had also noticed the changes, however Nicola's partner,* *Paul,* *refused to accept there was any difference and this was only increasing the tension between them all at the weekends. Nicola and Paul came to see me as they were becoming concerned that their relationship was really beginning to suffer.*

In our first session, we talked about how the couple felt at weekends. Clearly Nicola was becoming anxious as the access weekend approached, while Paul became more excited. Once the boys arrived, Paul recognised that he was apt to 'let them get away with things' much more than if they had been with him all the time. He wanted to enjoy their time together and as such avoided having to discipline them if at all possible. He then felt protective of them when Nicola attempted to instil house rules and this often resulted in arguments between the couple.

I began by explaining that their behaviour was really common and normal. All biological parents who have non-residential children have a desire to 'spoil' them when they visit and make the time together as 'perfect' as possible. Likewise, the stepparent in this case is often the one to enforce the rules – something they resent as it pushes them towards a role they are often largely uncomfortable with, particularly early on in their relationship.

Once Nicola and Paul realised that they had fallen into this pattern, they were both much more receptive to finding ways of improving the visits. By working with them together we were able to define some basic house rules that they both supported. Paul agreed that all the children (both his sons as well as his stepdaughter) needed to obey these basic rules and they agreed to support each other in disciplining the children as required. The couple were able to move forwards with more confidence.

Often the validation and normalisation stage facilitates more open and honest discussion. It allows the couple to relax and give each other the time and space to admit their self-perceived weaknesses and work with the therapist to find a way forward in the development of their family unit.

The following items are useful for therapists to discuss with stepfamilies when trying to normalise their feelings and behaviour. Often individuals are hugely relieved to find their feelings are normal and common within stepfamilies. From here they can then start to accept these feelings and build more constructive relationships within the family unit.

Normalising feelings and behaviour: topics to discuss

- There is no such thing as instant love.
- Stepfamilies develop and operate differently from first families.
- In successful stepfamilies, some members may be closer to some people than others.

- Most stepfamily members have experienced loss.
- Negotiation and conflict are normal and to be expected.
- Individuals in stepfamilies have different backgrounds.
- Children are often members of more than one household.
- There is likely to be an absent biological parent.
- For the stepparent, adopting an authority role takes time.
- Generally, older children find the transitions to stepfamily life more difficult and find it harder to accept their stepparent.

Establish realistic expectations

I really like my stepson but I can't stand my two stepdaughters. They are rude and difficult. I find it really hard making conversation with them both and they seem to gang up on me. They're always telling me how wonderful their mum is and what a fantastic cook she is. I feel I'm never going to measure up. I end up spending more and more time on my own in my bedroom. I feel miserable and resentful, and can't talk to my partner about it as I know he won't understand.

(Ella, September 2013)

Ella *came to see me for help in addressing some of the problems she was experiencing with her stepchildren. She had been living with her partner for a year and was at a loss as to what to do to next in terms of building her relationship with her stepchildren. She had forged a good bond with her stepson but was finding it increasingly difficult to develop any positive relationship with her stepdaughters. She felt she had tried in the past, but recognised that she was now changing her behaviour to avoid them whenever possible. This was beginning to impact on her relationship with her partner, who couldn't understand why things were seemingly getting worse and not better.*

This example illustrates a number of stepfamily realities. Often individuals have unrealistic expectations of stepfamily development, and this can impact on their ability to effectively move forward and develop the relationships.

Ella's stepson was only 6 when she first met him; her stepdaughters were aged 11 and 13. She immediately found it easier to bond with her stepson, looking after him and spending time with him when they came to visit. However, the girls seemed more reluctant to join in anything when they came to visit. They both wanted to spend time with their father and tended to ignore Ella. Their behaviour is quite typical of older, particularly teenage, children, who often find it more difficult to accept stepparents and take longer to transition into the stepfamily. In Ella's case, it became apparent that the girls were finding it difficult to accept their parents' separation and divorce. They were still mourning the loss of their family and did not feel ready to accept Ella as their stepmother.

In challenging some of Ella's expectations about stepfamily life, I was able to reassure her that her behaviour and thoughts were normal and rational. Children need time to adjust to changes in families, and some take longer than others. This can be affected both by the age and gender of the child, with older children sometimes resisting change. They can be still mourning the loss of their parents' relationship and the family life they have known. Teenage girls in particular can be very protective of their mothers and find it difficult to share precious time with their fathers, particularly if they don't see him frequently. I encouraged Ella to persevere with her relationships with her stepdaughters, spending more time as a family rather than letting them monopolise their father when they came to visit. As time progressed and Ella became more confident, she started spending time with the girls alone. She was able to reassure them that she understood how hard the transition was for them, and that she was not trying to replace their mum in any way.

In recognising why the girls were behaving in this way – and understanding that they were not being spiteful to her, but resisting change and dealing with the loss of their family – Ella was able to deal more effectively with her emotions and start to build a more positive relationship with the girls.

This example illustrates the types of issue that are exacerbated by individuals assuming unrealistic expectations about the development of the family. It is important for practitioners to challenge unrealistic expectations and replace them with more realistic, achievable goals. If this isn't done, the resultant discrepancy has been shown to lead to further issues, including increased depression and resentment. Indeed, research on all mothers, both step and biological, has shown that when their experiences did not match expectations, the women suffered from greater depression (Harwood, McLean and Durkin, 2007). Similarly, research involving stepfamilies has consistently found that stepmothers hold unrealistic expectations about their role (e.g. Orchard and Solberg, 1999; Weaver and Coleman, 2005), and this is a contributory factor to their overall mental wellbeing. Turning to young people and adolescents and their expectations of stepfamilies, research suggests that young people hold a conservative view of family relationships within stepfamilies, expecting the biological parent to maintain primary responsibility for the children and the stepparent to play a more minor role. This is particularly relevant in discipline issues, with many children expecting their parent to prioritise their needs over those of their parent's partner (Moore and Cartwright, 2005). Overall, findings therefore suggest that there are potentially diverse needs and expectations within the new stepfamily that can cause conflict and ongoing difficulties within the family if not addressed.

Table 3.2 lists a number of expectations together with the reality. Again working through this with stepfamily members helps reset their expectations, leading to more achievable goals and, ultimately, greater wellbeing.

Strengthen the couple bond and enhance communication

The couple relationship is the most important relationship in the new stepfamily as, without it, the stepfamily is no longer a family, but merely two independent biological units. The couple are the glue that holds the new family together. They do not replace the prior family but form the foundations of the new family unit. In order to build a strong, functioning stepfamily, the couple have to work together as a unit, holding similar views and values to ensure that the children within the family are treated fairly and equally. This area can require a lot of attention as the couple are divided on fundamental issues, often related to parenting and discipline. Indeed, Papernow (cited in Pryor, 2008) stressed the importance of professionals working with the new couple to strengthen their relationship and develop shared goals and values.

Clinical interventions to prevent or treat couple relationship problems in the context of stepfamilies are extremely limited. Much of the clinical work with stepfamilies has focused on stepparent–stepchild relationships, with little or no attention paid to the couple (Lawton

Table 3.2   Expectations vs reality

Expectation	Reality
All stepfamily members will get on with one another and form close bonds.	Stepparents and stepchildren will certainly not love each other at the start of the relationship – and may not even like each other. Couples need to be encouraged to foster an environment of mutual respect and care. No one should feel 'guilty' if they do not love their stepchildren and neither should stepchildren be expected to love their stepparents. However, as long as everyone shows respect within the household, the relationships can be left to develop naturally over time
We can replicate a biological family and be 'normal'	The majority of individuals entering a stepfamily often have a desire to replicate a biological family. Indeed some couples that go on to have children of their own within the stepfamily don't even think of themselves as a stepfamily. However it's important to recognise that stepfamilies have different challenges and demands from biological families, and to ignore this simply creates more discontent and frustration within the family
We will all get on with one another and have similar relationships	Some members of a stepfamily may be closer to one another than others. Within a biological family, parents rarely show overt favouritism, and love all their children equally. In stepfamilies, it is common for stepparents to feel closer to one stepchild than another. Often this is related to personality characteristics but may also be related to the gender and/or age of the children. It is important that the stepparents recognise this is normal but are given support in developing the best relationships they can with all family members, and ensure that all children within the family are treated equally and fairly
All stepfamily members will accept the new family structure and be prepared to get to know one another and move on	It is important to recognise that the majority of stepfamily members have experienced loss and will need time to adjust. The stepfamily is formed when the couple decide to formalise their relationship in some way, either by acknowledging the relationship to their children, physically moving in together or marrying. However, they are the ones setting the pace of change and others – the children and extended family and friends – often need more time to adjust. Frequently the children may still be coming to terms with the loss of their previous life, either with their biological parents together or living with one parent

(continued)

Table 3.2 Expectations vs reality (*continued*)

Expectation	Reality
We get on so well as a couple, we're bound to agree on most things in our new family	Negotiation and conflict are normal and to be expected. At least one adult in the relationship is already a parent and will have fixed views on how they want their relationship to continue with their children. Typically, they will hold different perspectives than their new partner, and the development of the new family unit will involve negotiation and compromise
We will set the rules and expect 'our' children to respect these, wherever they are	Children are often members of more than one household, where there will be different rules and expectations. Couples should recognise that they have 'control' only within their own household – children may have different rules and expectations outside their home. Many children spend time in both their mother's and father's households, meaning that the households are connected through the children. However, it is important that everyone maintains appropriate emotional and physical boundaries between the two homes to reinforce the separation. If this isn't maintained children can often fantasise that their parents will get back together again
Both adults in the stepfamily have equal control in the new stepfamily, regardless of whether they are the biological or stepparent	It is important in new stepfamilies that the biological parent takes the lead on issues related to discipline. The authority role for the stepparent therefore takes time to establish. Stepparents should concentrate on building a relationship based on respect with their stepchildren in the early stages of the new family development, taking their lead from the biological parent. Over time, they can start to take a more prominent position, but they must be encouraged not to rush into this role
All children will adapt to stepfamily life in the same way and with the same challenges	Different children have different challenges, and this can vary depending on the age and gender of the children. Generally, the older the children, the more difficult the transitions and the acceptance of the stepparent
The initial chaos of the new stepfamily will settle down quickly and we'll all just get on	The development and integration of a stepfamily typically takes several years and involves many stages in its development

and Sanders, 1994). However, it is important to note that general couple interventions (i.e. not related specifically to stepfamilies (e.g. Halford *et al.*, 2003)) are not likely to be effective if they do not address stepfamily-specific factors that confer additional risks (Whitton, Nicholson and Markman, 2008). A strong couple relationship is the key to a healthy stepfamily – if the couple are content and happy in their relationship they are much more able to support the family and deal with the problems that inevitably arise.

But, while this relationship is critical to the success of the stepfamily, it is also the most vulnerable as it is the newest family relationship; unfortunately they don't have the benefit of shared family history to strengthen their bonds. And, unlike first families, they don't have the luxury of time together as a couple before children come along.

Couple conflict and ineffective problem solving are strong predictors of marital distress and divorce for all couples (e.g. Clements, Stanley and Markman, 2004). Unfortunately problems in these areas appear to be more pronounced for stepfamily couples, with research showing them to be more negative, and less supportive, to have poorer problem-solving skills and be more likely to withdraw from discussions than biological couples (Bray and Berger, 1993; Halford, Nicholson and Sanders, 2007). Additionally, stepfamily couples have self reported that they avoid discussion of sensitive topics more than biological couples (Afifi and Schrodt, 2003). There is clearly significant evidence to suggest that there is less effective communication between couples in stepfamilies, which in turn predicts relationship dissatisfaction. Clinical interventions are therefore very valuable when focused on improving couples' conflict resolution skills.

Toolkit 3.1 Good times exercise

An exercise to help stepfamily members focus on positive memories or aspects of their family rather than dwelling on issues or problems.

Develop clear, unambiguous roles for the stepparent

Psychologists have for many years believed that the stress experienced by stepparents was in part caused by the absence of so-called

Table 3.3   Definition of stepparenting styles (Erera-Weatherley, 1996)

Stepparenting style	Profile
Birth parent style	Stepfathers who adopted this style (not adopted by stepmothers) believed that step and biological parenthood were identical and, as such, they behaved the same way to all their children, irrespective of relationship
The super good stepparent	These stepmothers (not demonstrated by stepfathers) went out of their way to be a good stepparent in order to dispel the wicked stepmother myth; their only aim was to be liked and appreciated by their stepchildren
The detached stepparent	These stepparents were minimally involved in their stepchildren's lives and the detachment tended to follow unsuccessful attempts to implement one of the more active stepparent styles; stepmothers in this category tended to be non-residential
The uncertain stepparent	These stepparents (frequently stepfathers) expressed doubt, uncertainty and distress in their role, seeking guidance and reassurance
The friendship style	Most stepparents adopting this non-parental style expressed a sense of genuine acceptance of the stepchildren and wanted to be a friend rather than a parent to their stepchild

'social norms', or role models, to help them define their role within their stepfamily. As the roles are so vague, it is difficult for stepparents to assess how well they are coping, leading to ever increasing confusion and anxiety. In an effort to understand this issue more fully, research has identified a number of alternative role models adopted with varying effectiveness by stepparents. Erera-Weatherley (1996) focused on developing stepfamily models based on the parenting style adopted by stepparents. A description of these types is presented in Table 3.3.

The study showed that these styles were developmental, with stepparents trying different styles before eventually adopting a preferred style. Of the five stepparenting styles identified in the study, the most effective – based on the accounts of both stepparents and their spouses – was the friendship style. The study found that stepmothers who attempted the super good stepparent style generally failed to set appropriate limits or enforce discipline, which resulted in resentment towards the stepchild and spouse. Further conflict was evident in stepparents who adopted the birth parent style, and the detached stepparent style led to animosity and alienation between the stepchild and the stepparent. Stepparents who adopted the uncertain style perceived more stress in the role and had weaker relationships with their stepchildren.

While there are no predefined roles, it is vital that both adults have the same expectations and understanding if the family is to develop successfully. Practitioners need to help the couple understand each other's perspectives and begin to develop a sense of their agreed roles within the family. There's no *one* parenting type that works best, although some do seem to offer better outcomes to most stepfamilies.

Toolkit 3.2 Understanding your role in the stepfamily

A description of the more common stepparenting roles is given at the end of the chapter. This can be discussed with clients or given to them to read as 'homework'.

Set clear boundaries for the ongoing relationship and communication with ex partners

My own research on stepmothers (Doodson, 2014) identified significant anxiety related to the biological mothers. Stepmothers spoke of their frustration and jealousy at the enduring relationship that they could never hope to equal. The mother was always portrayed as a positive role model for the children, irrespective of the actual role they played in their children's lives. Many also struggled with the loss of control they felt in their own household, with biological parents often exerting control over the stepparents either directly or indirectly. For example, many would not be allowed to pick up their stepchildren from school, or would be told what the children could or couldn't eat. This served to reinforce their role as inferior in some way to the biological parents. Related research on the relationship between control and mental wellbeing has provided evidence that, for new parents, impairment in control is associated with depression, stress and anxiety-related disorders (Shapiro, Schwartz and Astin, 1996; Chorpita and Barlow, 1998; Mirowsky and Ross, 1999; Keeton, Perry-Jenkins and Sayer, 2008). Consequently, when new stepparents experience this lack of control they are more susceptible to heightened depression and anxiety.

While it is recognised that a parenting coalition of parents and step-parents is often beneficial for both adults and children (Visher and Visher, 1996) it is not always easy to establish this in the early stages of the new stepfamily. It is therefore important that practitioners work with the new couple to define clear boundaries, with a view of working towards a more co-operative relationship between the biological parents over time. If the separation was acrimonious, and there is ongoing anger and resentment, it is unlikely that a collaborative relationship can be established. In this case the adults should be encouraged to set clear boundaries between the households and help the new couple communicate more effectively in this area. Where the relationships are fraught and remain antagonistic, the aim is to keep communication to a minimum and focused solely on making arrangements for the children. Individuals should be encouraged to avoid engaging in any further discussion as this is likely to maintain the emotional responses. The biological parent needs to be reminded to consider the impact of any decisions they make on their partner and keep them updated with any unavoidable changes to plans. When working with the stepparent, therapists need to remind them that successful stepfamilies have to maintain flexibility as plans are not always within their sole control. They should also keep talking to their partner about any concerns or anxieties they have related to the ex partner. In this way, its hoped that anxiety related to ex partners can be reduced, so enabling the ongoing development of the new family unit.

The integrated approach

The interventions identified in the previous section are fundamental to all stepfamily development and integration. However, I believe that in order to be able to support a wide range of families effectively it is important to consider alternative methods of delivery that vary depending on the specific needs and dynamics within the family. Figure 3.1 illustrates the three components of Integrated Stepfamily Therapy and shows how an integrated approach to stepfamily therapy can offer targeted interventions to a wide client base.

If therapists can consider and draw on skills involving this triad of approaches they are more likely to address the wider needs of stepfamilies. These approaches are introduced below and will be explored and described in detail in the following chapters.

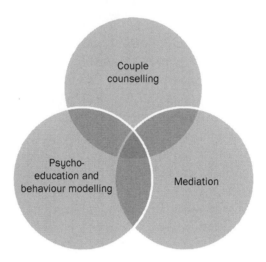

Figure 3.1 Integrated Stepfamily Therapy

Couple counselling

This type of intervention is most suited to couples who are at a particular crisis in their relationship. Often they have been dealing with the difficulties in their family structure for some time and are both exhausted in trying to find a way forward. While many of the issues they are presenting are common to stepfamilies, they need one-to-one support to help them prioritise the issues and work together to identify solutions.

Psycho-education and behaviour modelling

For many couples, particularly at the start of their relationship, education is the primary goal. They are often overwhelmed by the challenges of stepfamily life, and need help in putting together the structure and foundation of their new family. For these couples, education can often best be provided in a group setting. This allows couples to understand the main challenges that stepfamilies face and to learn how to cope more effectively with the difficulties. They are also able to meet other couples in a similar situation. This helps reinforce the normality of their situation: couples realise that their issues are common and often shared among other couples. It also helps to reinforce the messages that are delivered throughout the course. Often the couples are able to then initiate their own 'self help' support group, meeting independently to share problems and, more importantly, solutions.

Mediation

Often, working with couples in stepfamilies can be frustrating. As a practitioner you may often feel that the wrong people are sitting in front of you. All too frequently, the main issues appear to be entrenched between the biological parents rather than the couple from the stepfamily. The stepfamily couple, however, is left to deal with the inevitable fallout resulting from issues primarily outside their control. However, if you can identify a common goal between the biological couple – perhaps a desire to finalise holiday arrangements or agreement on Christmas plans, it might be possible to suggest mediation. We are becoming used to seeing mediation used as a recognised approach when couples separate or divorce, however I believe it can also play a vital part in resolving ongoing issues. This method is described in more detail in Chapter 6.

Integrating the therapy

Often a single approach is appropriate for couples: some will benefit from psycho-educational group workshops and will then feel they have the tools to move on with the development of their family, while others will need one-to-one support and may remain in therapy for several sessions as they address the most pressing issues. However, it may be appropriate to signpost couples to alternative therapies. Sometimes mediation may be used alongside one-to-one coaching. Other couples may find benefit in the workshop after seeking help with specific issues in one-to-one therapy, or vice versa. Practitioners may also need to consider signposting to general parenting courses, or perhaps even offering therapy or counselling to individuals to address issues outside of the stepfamily dynamic.

Conclusion and key learning points

This chapter has shown how the unique problems experienced by stepfamilies demand a different approach from professionals. Treating these families in the same way as biological families often fails to address the most pressing issues that the family is experiencing. However, I challenge practitioners to consider exploring different methods of delivering the interventions, not limited to stepfamily couple therapy, but considering group workshops and mediation, or even a combination of these approaches in order to reach all potential clients effectively.

Toolkit

This toolkit contains exercises that have been designed to support relationship professionals in their work with stepfamilies.

3.1   Good times exercise

Sometimes, as stepparents or stepchildren in a family, we can get very involved and drawn into what's going wrong in our lives. And sometimes we discount or forget about the nice moments and the peaceful or enjoyable times we are having. This exercise invites every member of the family to notice moments in the week when they felt good. It could be that you laughed at something funny on the TV or you went for a peaceful walk in the rain. It could be about nice things that you did for others, or they did for you. It could be something really, really small that made you happy. Please can you write about this in as much detail as you like, just concentrating on what it was that made you happy. No negative bits, only happy moments and feel free to describe things using colours and vivid language. If you prefer, you can draw a picture ... or write this down. Then share your happy moment with others in the family.

3.2   Understanding your role in the stepfamily

Ask the stepparent to try to define their role in the family. For example, do they feel they are like a parent or perhaps they feel more of a friend to their stepchildren. Ask them also to think about what activities they share *with* their stepchildren and what kind of things they do *for* them.

The following describes stepparenting roles commonly adopted by individuals taking on the role within a stepfamily. These are by no means the only role models, however they are worth discussing with couples as they highlight the potential benefits and issues associated with each model.

The third parent

Many people believe that step and biological parenting are identical and, as such, they try to behave and feel exactly the same towards their stepchildren as they would their own children. They see this as logical and natural. By treating their stepchildren in this way, stepparents are less likely to experience any role ambiguity as they are clear about their role as a 'parent' to their stepchildren. This can make life easier for both the stepparent and the rest of the family. The difficulties in this style lie in the potential conflicts if the stepchildren don't accept their stepparent in this way. This could lead to the stepparent feeling rejected, and becoming resentful and angry at the situation. There could also be further conflict between the stepparent and their partner if they don't agree on the stepparent taking such an active role in parenting of the children.

However, this can be a really positive role for a stepparent to adopt, as long as everyone in the family unit is in agreement. If the stepparent feels that they view themselves as an 'extra' parent then it's important that the stepchildren understand that they're not simply trying to 'replace' their other parent. People who have been successful in adopting this approach have generally tried to build some form of relationship with their stepchildren's 'other parent', to enable them to share information and make the transition between homes easier for everyone.

The 'super stepparent'

These stepparents go out of their way to be seen to be conscientious stepparents to their stepchildren. It is typically a role adopted by stepmothers rather than stepfathers. Many adopt this style to try to dispel the myth of the wicked stepmother, and typically shower their stepchildren with love, affection and material gifts. They often avoid telling their stepchildren off, leaving this job to their partner. They want to prove to themselves and their partner that they can do a good job, and they want to 'win round' the children. This can be successful but it's important that stepparents realise they can't always be superman or superwoman! The children need time to get to know them. Everyone needs to know when they have let someone down or done something wrong so that they can change their behaviour – otherwise they're likely to keep doing it. The danger with this approach is that the stepchildren can start to take advantage of the stepparent. Many parents who adopt this style avoid setting boundaries or disciplining their stepchildren, in an effort to be popular. But if this approach doesn't work, and the stepchildren fail to show their appreciation for the stepparent, this can lead to resentment towards the children and even the partner.

The 'backseat' stepparent

People who identify with this style have minimal involvement with their stepchildren. They tend to leave things to their partners. For example, when their stepchildren come to stay they make their (polite) excuses and go and visit friends. They don't dislike their stepchildren, but they don't feel they have a bond with them either. As far as they are concerned, their partner's children are just that, and they take a backseat. They see themselves as supportive to their partner but want to give their partner time to spend with their children – alone. This approach can work in some cases, particularly where the parent doesn't see their children very frequently and wants to spend as much time as possible with them. The difficulties, however, often occur when the couple haven't assumed these roles but it has become the default approach. This style is usually adopted after stepparents have failed to make one of the other styles work for them. For example, some people may start off trying to be the super stepparent, however when their efforts aren't appreciated or they feel rejected, they can feel alienated and develop a distance from their stepchildren in an effort to minimise their hurt. Although it can be successful, particularly if the children don't visit regularly, or perhaps are older, it can lead to feelings of isolation.

The 'unsure' stepparent

These stepparents are unsure of their position or role in the family, and need reassurance and help. It is usually a style adopted by individuals who have no parenting experience and feel overwhelmed by their new-found responsibilities. They are unsure how to 'parent' their stepchild, and seek help from their partner in setting boundaries and rules. This style is more likely to increase anxiety for stepparents and can make it harder for them to develop close relationships with their stepchildren.

The 'friend'

This style is adopted by people who don't want to be a parental figure to their stepchildren. They develop close relationships with their stepchildren but accept that they will never replace the biological parents in their affections. This style seems to be particularly effective when the stepchildren have a close relationship with their other biological parent, as there is less comparison between the roles. It also seems to engender greater openness and trust between the stepparent and stepchildren, and has been shown to be the most common style adopted by stepmothers. However, it is worth pointing out that it's easier to adopt this style when the stepchildren are a little bit older – toddlers don't really need adult friends, they need carers and parents. It is important to remember though that, even as a friend, stepparents need to be clear on house rules.

It is essential to remind the couple that there is no right or wrong approach. The important thing is to identify the style that most closely resembles the role the stepparent is most comfortable with. Research has suggested that while stepparents broadly adopt one of these roles, they generally gravitate to one after having attempted other approaches. So, over time, stepparents who are uncertain about their role develop more confidence. They develop closer relationships with their stepchildren and may begin to identify more closely with the friendship style. Conversely, those that try to adopt a close, parenting style early on in the relationship may find that they need to step back and take things more slowly.

Advice for stepparents in adopting a role model

1. Work out what it is you want to be and what type of role you want in your family.
2. Understand your partner's perspective.
3. Are your views similar or do they differ? If they differ, try to understand why. Perhaps your partner is taking into consideration the views of their children as well?
4. Work out the major differences and try to compromise. It is important that both of you consider all family members, particularly the children.
5. Once you have reached agreement, try to stick to it! You can always review things over time. Nothing is fixed for ever but, for now, work together on establishing the roles that you've agreed on for your family.

4 COUPLE COUNSELLING

The previous chapter introduced the model for Integrated Stepfamily Therapy (IST), which comprises three components: couple counselling, psycho-education and behaviour modelling and mediation. This chapter describes how this model is applied to the first of these approaches: couple counselling. The questions being addressed are therefore as follows.

- How can practitioners use IST to help stepfamilies develop more effectively?
- What are the individual stages involved?
- What information should practitioners capture and how can they then use this to help the couple in the development and integration of their family?

The background

The approach is based on two assumptions that underpin the model. First, that if stepfamily-related issues are addressed, the family will be able to move on independently with the development of their family unit. The assumption is based on the principle that there are a range of normal reactions to the adjustments of becoming a stepfamily and that the issues being experienced by the presenting couple are as a result of the stepfamily dynamics. In essence they are a 'normal' stepfamily and, if the issues are addressed, the couple can move on independently of external support. However, if the issues are primarily related to areas unrelated to the stepfamily development then the couple are more likely to benefit from alternative therapeutic approaches. Second, that stepfamilies need solution-focused support to help them cope with issues related to stepfamily development. The approach is a practical, goal-driven model, with an emphasis on developing clear and concise plans. The aim is to work with clients to help them develop realistic goals focused on addressing their key stepfamily related issues. The aim is to give enough support to clients to help them address the problems they are currently facing in the development of their stepfamily. Often the couple are then able to move on independently, utilising the tools they have received from the practitioner. They may return at a later date presenting different issues, due to evolving relationships within the stepfamily, however the time between sessions allows them to move forwards with the family integration. The break between sessions is therefore healthy and to be encouraged.

The model is underpinned with these assumptions and firmly rooted in the framework of key interventions, focused on healthy stepfamily development. Many of these interventions (see Table 3.1) will be common to the majority of couples in stepfamilies and should be addressed as part of the therapy. It may be that not all interventions are required by all couples, however it is up to the therapist to assess the specific needs and ensure all the key areas are addressed. The following section discusses each of these potential interventions.

Stages of the therapeutic model

The model comprises four stages that practitioners are encouraged to follow. While all families have different priorities and demands, research and clinical experience has shown that all couples can benefit from receiving support and advice utilising the following stages and interventions.

1. Initial assessment – develop comprehensive family background
2. Prioritise issues – challenges preventing couple from moving forwards
3. Identify solutions – compromises or alternative approaches to address issues
4. Homework – to reinforce the work completed in sessions

Stage 1: Initial assessment

The purpose of the initial meeting is to understand more about the family dynamics and relationships, and to identify the issues that have brought the clients to therapy. It is generally accepted that it is preferable at this stage for the therapist to see both the adults in the stepfamily together, to hear both perspectives and identify any different expectations or needs.

It is more usually the biological mother or stepmother who makes the first appointment, but regardless of which individual initially seeks the support it is important to encourage them to come to the appointment with their partner. However, often this doesn't happen and only one adult is prepared to seek the help they feel they need. In this case I recommend that the professional proceed with the assessment but also encourages the client to tell their partner about the appointment and suggest joint sessions as appropriate once the therapy has begun. I would also advise against including children or stepchildren at this point. This allows parents to speak openly and give a complete history, including information about former partners and their relationships.

It's important to note here that the goal of this initial session is to identify the key challenges for this family and to confirm that this approach will be of benefit. It may be that during this assessment it becomes clear that the primary issues are unrelated to stepfamily issues, in which case they should be referred to alternative therapy and support as appropriate. The aim is to gather as much information about the stepfamily as possible in this session. Often the meeting can be quite chaotic as the couple find themselves able to vocalise their feelings and issues for the first time in what may have been a long time. It is the role of the therapist to guide the couple to provide a clear explanation of the family membership and the underlying issues that are causing the current difficulties.

The following section provides an outline of the type of information that needs to be gathered from the client.

Family description

The primary goal here is to gather as much relevant information about the family composition as possible. Specifically, the therapist needs to understand not just the immediate family, but the wider family relationships, including grandparents, siblings, ex partners – and relationships that they may have developed, which may also include further children. Often this can become quite complex but it is essential in helping the therapist understand some of the pressures being exerted on the stepfamily.

The most obvious way to capture this information is by using a 'genogram'. A genogram, first used by family therapists, is a pictorial display of an individual's family relationships. It goes beyond a traditional family tree by allowing the user to visualise hereditary patterns and psychological factors that affect relationships. Although there are many systems that can be used, there is general uniformity on the symbols used to identify gender, marriage, separation, etc. Systems used for expressing relationships (e.g. good, enmeshed, distant) tend to vary. I therefore encourage therapists to use the method they are already familiar with. I would recommend McGoldrick, Gerson and Petry's *Genograms: Assessment and Intervention* (2008) for a detailed description of genograms and the associated legend. Often this is the first opportunity a couple has to share their problems and it is vital that this detail isn't lost amid the desire to create a genogram. It may be that the genogram develops over time – that's fine, the most important goal of this first session is for the therapist to begin to capture the main problems that the couple are experiencing.

As such, the aim is to listen to the client in order to identify and capture any external influences on the family and to develop a thorough representation of the wider family relationships. Stepfamilies are, by their nature, more complex than biological families and it is important to find a way to visually represent these complexities, and use this to probe and identify potential areas for future focus. The therapist should continue to build on the genogram as the sessions continue and use it as a basis for prioritising the focus of help. It's important to also identify any difficulties in relationships identified within the genogram.

As part of the family composition, it is essential that the therapist identify the stepfamily type at this stage. Specifically it is important to recognise both the complexity (i.e. do one or both individuals have prior children?) and the residency of all the children. Children may reside with the couple on a permanent basis or may visit. There may also be different schedules for the different children within the family, with not all children spending the same amount of time within the stepfamily.

Ensure the following information is captured.

● Include members of immediate family (adults and children, step and biological) and the strength of each relationship. Ensure that all children are captured – whether they live with the couple or not. I have known some couples leave out children if they no longer visit them. It is not unusual to find that there are different allegiances between the children.

- Include ex partners and any new relationships they may have formed, and include any children that may be part of these unions (biological and stepchildren). Identify the strength of these relationships and any ongoing issues. It is particularly important here to identify any reasons for change. For example, an ex partner may well have just remarried or moved in with their partner who also has prior children. This can often affect the sometimes fragile co-parenting arrangements, with individuals trying to change access arrangements to better meet their new family structure and needs.
- Include the relationship between the children in the family to capture the strength of the relationship between step and half siblings as necessary. You may, for example, find that biological children will stick together against the incoming stepchildren, making it very difficult for the latter to feel welcome and at home.
- Capture extended family, including siblings and parents of the couple. This is important to understanding the level of support they receive and can rely on. Identify any issues such as acceptance of the stepparent or ongoing loyalty to ex partners. Grandparents, for example, can be a blessing for stepfamilies when they offer support and fair treatment of all the children, however a doting grandparent who favours their own biological grandchildren can create lots of issues within the stepfamily.

Timeline

Once the basic family structure has been established, the therapist needs to establish a timeline. Not only is it important to understand how long the couple have been in the relationship but also how long they have been living together and when changes occurred in their relationship. For example, it is not uncommon for couples to spend several years as a couple but living separately before moving in together. The therapist needs to establish when the couple met, when children were introduced to partners, when the couple moved in together and, if relevant, when they subsequently married. It is also important to include on the timeline when they each separated from previous partners and how long those relationships lasted, or how long they were single prior to the present relationship.

Relationships that have developed swiftly following the termination of previous relationships can often mean that individuals are still grieving for the losses. While the adults may have moved on, children or wider family members may still be coming to terms with the recent changes, which clearly affects the development of the new family. Similarly, if one partner has had multiple relationships, the children may be reluctant to invest time in getting to know the new partner, fearing that the relationship may not last.

Children who have lived alone with a single parent for many years will fight to retain their status should the parent meet a new partner. Often, single parents give their children a more adult role in the relationship – boys become the 'man' in the household for their mothers, daughters enjoy the affection often bestowed on them by single fathers. These acquired roles make it extremely difficult for stepparents to be accepted within the new stepfamily, with an often prolonged period of readjustment of roles and status.

Co-parenting arrangements

Another key area to focus on is the arrangement the couple have with the absent biological parent. This may be for one or both adults depending on the complexity of the stepfamily. Within this often complex area, the therapist needs to identify what arrangements currently exist for co-parenting of the children. For example, are these arrangements formally constructed through a court or are they more informal? Do they tend to be fixed or is there flexibility depending on the needs of the parents and the children? It is important to understand both the history – were the arrangements acrimonious, involving lengthy legal interventions, or was agreement met quite amicably and relatively painlessly? – as well as the present arrangements. While many couples spend time and finances hammering out custody arrangements over time these can evolve, with changes triggered by a variety of causes. For example, a change in personal circumstances such a new job or a new partner can affect a parent's ability, and sometimes desire, to care for their children within the agreed pattern. As children grow they can express a desire to change the contact arrangements themselves – for example, teenage boys often enjoy spending more time with their fathers, and it's not unusual to witness problems arising in stepfamilies caused by these changes. The changes in custody arrangements can often be subtle, with ad hoc requests from the other parent, or even the child themselves, becoming more frequent over time, resulting in significant differences between the agreement and the actual weekly arrangements. It is important that the therapist identify any changes over time as these can be trigger points to current issues within the family. For example, a stepparent who believed that their stepchildren would be visiting every other weekend can sometimes struggle to cope when they find themselves as the main carer months or years later.

Turning to the visits themselves, it is important for the therapist to understand the mechanics. How does the transfer take place? Are the children collected from home, school or, as is sometimes the case, a neutral location to avoid conflict? Do the biological parents facilitate this or are stepparents involved? I have had many cases, for example, where the biological parent refuses to let their ex partner's new partner (the stepparent) pick up their child from school. This can cause both physical issues for the parent, who may not be able to pick up their child due to work commitments, together with frustration and anger from the stepparent.

Often the therapist will find that the responsibility of child pick-ups and drop-offs are left with one parent, with the other biological parent playing no active role. This can also lead to conflict and arguments between the parent who has to carry out this activity and their partner.

One of my clients was left at breaking point on this issue. They lived about a 90-minute car journey from their children (aged 6 and 9 years old) who they saw every other weekend. Every other Friday they would drive for three hours to pick them up from their mother's house. The handover would often be tearful, with the mother breaking down at the children leaving. The father then spent the remaining journey trying to calm the children down and reassuring them that their mummy would be fine without them. On arriving home, the father wanted nothing more than to spend some time relaxing with the children while his partner wanted to bundle them off to bed! Sometimes the mother would also contact the father during the week and inform him that the children had some event planned during the weekend which they were looking forward to and didn't want to miss – for example, a friend's party or a sports event. This would often mean he had to either pick up the children later on the Saturday or drop them off earlier on the Sunday. The stepmum was very frustrated that their weekends were punctuated by these trips and being further dictated by the actions of the biological mum. The couple had a very young child together so the constant changes to plans were affecting the time the whole family could spend together.

In this instance it was important to set boundaries between the biological parents, as well as rules regarding weekend access. The father asked his ex partner to stop planning activities for the children on his access weekends, leaving him to make decisions for the weekend with his partner. This wasn't straightforward as often the children were invited to friends' parties and he was reluctant to let them down. However, I helped him realise that it should be his decision to make and to then explain to the children, rather than letting things continue unchecked.

Finally, the issues of maintenance should be discussed. I tend to find that individuals will often discount this issue with comments such as 'Oh, it's not about the money – it's the principle', but frequently it plays a significant part in tension within the new couple. In the UK it is very common for one parent to pay maintenance for the child or children to the other parent who has primary care. In some cases they also have to pay maintenance for their ex partner. Sometimes the maintenance itself causes flashpoints – for example, if there is a change in circumstances in either family or perhaps a desire for the new couple to start a family. Frequently couples will vent their frustrations in sessions that they are paying significant money to ex spouses when they themselves are struggling financially. Often the issue is not with the maintenance itself but in the additional costs that are borne. For example, parents who pay maintenance can find themselves agreeing to pay for further trips, holidays, clothes or other items for their children. This can be extremely contentious with their partners, who feel that they are already providing support. Often the parent feels stuck in the middle, not wanting to let their children down or perhaps avoiding ongoing conflict with their ex, together with finding agreement with their partner.

These distinct but related areas should all be explored in order to identify trigger points within the stepfamily, which can then be addressed within the therapy.

Relationships and roles

It is important that the therapist takes time to explore the multiple relationships and roles within the family, as these are often the source of ongoing conflict within the new stepfamily (see Chapter 3 for details on alternative role definitions for stepparents).

Couple relationship

As we have already discussed, the couple's relationship is the lynchpin of the stepfamily; without this relationship the stepfamily would not exist. It is therefore essential that this relationship is nurtured and strengthened. The therapist should assess the couple's communication patterns and key pressure points. Are they supportive of each other? Is the relationship conflictual? What are their individual coping strategies? Do they have similar goals and expectations? Are they willing to compromise? The role of the therapist here is to encourage the couple to work together on the problems and to try to seek compromise where possible. There is probably also a degree of setting realistic expectations for both parties and encouraging open and positive communication.

Relationship between biological parents and respective households

One of the biggest issues stepfamilies often have to face is in dealing with problems that are not within their own sphere of control. All too frequently I see couples who are despairing over their relationship with their ex partner. It's important to be able to gauge the level of ongoing conflict. When communicating, for example, are the couple able to talk rationally and find compromise, or do the discussions always end up as arguments? How does the communication work? Face to face or perhaps via other media? Do the stepparents get involved in an effort to reduce the conflict or is communication only via the biological parents? The role of the therapist here is first to understand any difficulties within this relationship, and then help the couple recognise what they can and can't change. If, for example, the ex partner is intent on causing problems for the new couple due to ongoing bitterness and resentment, then the clients need advice on limiting the interactions with the ex and keeping clearly to any formal access arrangements. Obviously the therapist sees only one side of the story – the ex partner may well bring a different perspective. If the main issues being presented by the clients appear to be related to this area I would then recommend considering mediation between the biological parents. This is particularly helpful if the ongoing issues are related to access for the children. The mediation model for use with families is explained in Chapter 6.

Adults and children

The therapist needs to begin to understand the relationships that exist between both biological parents and their children, and between stepparents and stepchildren. Research has shown us that both types of relationship can be fraught and difficult, particularly when the relationships are developing in the early stages of the family development. Often if a biological parent sees their children for only short periods of time – for example, at weekends and holidays – they can feel guilty that they aren't around all the time for their children. They may then try to compensate by showering them with gifts and feeling unable to discipline them appropriately, worrying that if they do tell their children off they won't want to come and stay. It is only natural for them to feel this way but they need to understand that in order to provide appropriate boundaries for their children they need to have clear household rules and be consistent in their use of discipline. If parents behave this way it can cause further issues with their partner and their biological children, who may feel that rules are applied unfairly and unequally between the children. Fairness between children is vital in all families, however in stepfamilies it is even more important that children feel they are being treated the same. Biological parents can also feel guilty when they are being expected to parent their stepchildren all the time when their own biological children live elsewhere for the majority of the time. This can impact on the development of their relationship. For example, research has shown that stepparents who are also a biological parent find it more difficult to bond with their stepchildren and the relationships take longer to develop (Doodson, 2014). It is also important to identify when a biological parent is finding it hard to let their child maintain a good relationship with their ex partner. Do they interrogate their children when they return from a visit? Do they speak negatively about their ex partner in front of the children? Do they rely on the children to pass messages between the adults? None of these makes for a healthy relationship and all should of course be discouraged, however it is rare for individuals to acknowledge they are behaving in this way. I find it helpful to use literature to help educate couples, perhaps as take-home reading between sessions.

In terms of stepparents and stepchildren the problems can be quite extensive and broad. Therapists need to bear in mind the type of step-family (discussed extensively in earlier chapters) as this can impact the types of issue commonly experienced. Stepparents who don't have their own biological children frequently struggle to adapt to the role easily, feeling overwhelmed by and confused about their role within the family. Their lack of parenting experience, and often unrealistic expectations of the children and their own feelings, means that they are more likely to experience difficulties. Stepparents who are already bio-logical parents, however, face different hurdles. For these individuals, the parenting role is one that they are already comfortable in holding, however they often face conflict in parenting both their own biological children and their stepchildren. Research has found that they feel guilty in sharing their time and affection, often leading to a prolonged period of adjustment to the role.

Between the children

Dynamics between the children in the household can often be a fur-ther source of conflict that the developing stepfamily has to manage. This is particularly relevant to complex stepfamilies where both adults bring prior children into the new family unit, and can be further com-plicated by the birth of children. It is important for professionals to explore these relationships as they can have a significant impact on the overall wellbeing of the family. Parents naturally feel protective of their own biological children, particularly in the early stages of the new family development. If they feel that their child is not being wel-comed into the household by their partner's children, or sense unfair-ness in their treatment, then this can become a source of ongoing stress between the couple. Some of these issues are often difficult for the couple to manage as the children may be spending some of their time in another household. So while they may endeavour to be fair to all the children in their care, the children may well have very different experiences in their respective 'other' homes. For example, a couple who both have prior children may treat all their children fairly within the household, however when their children visit their other biological parents their experiences may be vastly different. Those differences are outside their control, however the impact may well be felt within the family unit as the children experience feelings of envy, jealousy or anger towards their stepsiblings.

Anne and Steve came to see me with such an issue. They had three children between them – Anne had a son aged 15, and Steve had two daughters aged 17 and 10. Anne's son lived all the time with Anne and Steve, and rarely saw his father. When Steve had initially separated from his ex partner five years previously, both his daughters had lived with their mother and visited Steve every other weekend and holidays, however for the past year the youngest daughter had been living with Steve and Anne full-time after a serious argument with her mother. She did still visit her mother but the majority of her time was spent with Steve and Anne. This change meant that Katy, the 17 year old, was the only child now spending only part of her time with Steve and Anne. The last year had been very difficult for the couple and Anne in particular was incredibly stressed. She was finding it increasingly difficult to engage with Katy and found herself dreading her visits. She found Katy very awkward and confrontational, constantly comparing Anne negatively to her mother and criticising just about everything she did. Her presence in the house also had a negative affect on her younger sister, who seemed to side with her elder sister when she was visiting, making things even more difficult for Anne. In trying to avoid conflict Anne found that she was withdrawing from engaging with her stepdaughter more and more, even though she realised this was not a good long-term solution. As she withdrew, Katy spent more time with her father, causing Anne to feel even more resentful and angry. Steve however was reluctant to step in. He felt very much trapped in the middle. While he was enjoying the time with his daughter he was worried about Anne. He was struggling to know how to change the dynamic between Anne and Katy without pushing Katy away.

Through our discussions it became apparent that Katy was finding it difficult to find her place within the family. At her mother's house she was now effectively an only child for the majority of time. Her mother was confiding in her and treating her as more of a friend than a daughter. However, at Anne and Steve's she was one of three 'children'. While she was the eldest child and approaching adulthood, Steve and Anne did not recognise her status as an emerging adult and treated her in much the same way as the other two children. The family had also recently moved house and Katy had been given the smallest bedroom, which was downstairs and therefore remote from the rest of the family.

Clearly this was the logical decision, given that the other children were permanent members of the family, however Katy had clearly been very unhappy with the decision, even though she understood the reasons. I felt that Katy's behaviour was related to her feelings of insecurity in their family, and her desire to be treated in a way that would recognise her age and status in the family. I suggested that rather than withdrawing from the relationship, Anne start to make more effort to spend time with Katy. I also encouraged her to start asking Katy for more help – for example, in preparing meals or helping with the younger children.

I worked with Anne and Steve to identify small changes they might make. For example, Anne asked Katy if she would like to go shopping to get ideas for redecorating her bedroom. Spending time together – without Steve – was something that they hadn't really done in the past. However, it was a way of showing Katy that they valued her opinion and also broke the pattern of Katy only ever spending time with Steve and seeking his opinion. Anne also started asking her to help out with cooking, particularly when she was going to be working late. I encouraged both Anne and Steve to be consistent in picking Katy up when she was being critical or hurtful. I helped Steve see that this could be done fairly informally and he didn't have to be frightened of engaging in these conversations.

Over a period of weeks the changes began to make a difference to the dynamics in the household. Anne felt more confident of her own position and as such, was prepared to allow Katy more responsibility. Their relationship was improving and had become much less hostile.

This case study illustrates how a perceived lack of fairness between children in a stepfamily can significantly impact all relationships within the family. Sadly, the presenting relationship issue becomes the focus of the family and other relationships that are developing will get forgotten. It is important to encourage the couple to recognise their successes as well as some of the challenges, to build a more balanced picture and raise their confidence levels.

Table 4.1 describes some of the most common issues that children may experience in stepfamilies.

The following list provides questions that should be considered as part of the initial assessment. It may be easiest to let the couple talk informally and just prompt them to fill in some gaps, however it is important to flesh out this information as soon as possible.

Table 4.1   Issues that children may experience in stepfamilies

A child's order in a family	A child's birth order may be very different between households. They could for example be a single child in one family and youngest in another. This can make it difficult for children to transition between their homes, with different expectations placed on them
Different ages	Spouses' children may well be very different in terms of age. This makes integration difficult to achieve as they will want/need very different things from their parents. For example, older children may be expected to look after younger stepsiblings, or similar-aged children may be expected to play and get on with the other children
Different genders	Even if the children are similar ages, if they are of different genders parents may find they have less in common and as such the integration is more prolonged and less intensive
How long were they on their own with their biological parent prior to this relationship?	Children who have lived for a period of time with one parent will often have developed a very exclusive relationship and will therefore resent and reject any change that challenges that relationship or requires them to start sharing, either emotionally or physically
Do they have step or half siblings with their other parent?	There may well be further relationships in other households that the children have to maintain and develop. These may well 'spill over' into the current household if they are problematic
What responsibilities do the children have?	Do the children all have similar responsibilities in the household? Are these age dependent or do they vary depending on other criteria? Are the responsibilities likely to differ between households?

(continued)

Table 4.1 Issues that children may experience in stepfamilies (*continued*)

Do all the children have their own space within the home? Is this equal for all children or are there differences depending on residency or relationship?	Stepfamilies by their nature often have to accommodate more children than biological families. This can make it very difficult for couples to ensure that all children have their own bedrooms. However, it is important for all the children to know that they have their own space within a bedroom, which might be shared, and that their possessions are kept safe for them when they are not at the house. Are visiting children treated differently to residential children? While it is understandable to give priority in terms of space to children who live in the home permanently, it is equally important that visiting children are made to feel welcome and included
What happens when children come to visit? Do they have to bring possessions/clothes with them?	There are no hard-and-fast rules – some children tend to travel between their homes with their own clothes and possessions, others have plenty of choice at both homes. The situation can differ depending on the ages and needs of the children, and the agreement in place between the parents. However, it is important to understand whether this area is a cause of conflict and to identify potential changes

1. How long have they been together as a couple?
2. Do they currently live together? If so, for how long?
3. Do they live in a former 'marital' house or is this a new home for them?
4. How and when did previous relationships end?
5. How long have they been single prior to this relationship?
6. Have either of them had to move a house/job to maintain the relationship?
7. How much support do they get from family and friends?
8. Who has children from prior relationships?
9. What are the ages and sex of the children?

10. Do the children get on with their own siblings/stepsiblings?
11. How well do the biological parents get on with each other?
12. What are the arrangements for access for the children?
13. Are these enforced by a court order, or more informal?
14. When do the children come to stay and for how long?
15. Is access formal or flexible?
16. Can changes be instigated easily or are the patterns fixed?
17. What are the arrangements for maintenance for children/ex partner?
18. Are these agreed or is this a source of ongoing contention?
19. How well do the stepparents get on with their stepchildren?
20. In terms of ex partners, have they re-partnered and, if so, how long ago?
21. Have the ex partners had any more biological children or stepchildren?

Stage 2: Prioritise issues

Once this basic information has been gathered it is then important to ask the couple what they are hoping to get from the sessions. In Brief Therapy this is often termed the 'magic question'. For example, what would be different in your life if we addressed the issue that's troubling you? How would it feel?

In terms of stepparents I often ask them:

> If I had a magic wand, what issues would you like me to fix in your family?

This helps them focus of the main problems as they see them – it may be realistic, such as 'I want a better relationship with my stepchildren', or completely unrealistic – 'I want my stepchildren to disappear from my life' – however their answer will help you gauge both the area of the problem and the depth of the issue. If both adults are present I ask both of them to give me an answer and ask their partner to remain silent while each one of them talks. In this way, you can clearly understand if there is a common issue that they both perceive as a difficulty, or whether they may have different objectives and perceptions of the dynamics of the family.

Encourage the couple to be as honest as they can here, as this is critical to the focus and ultimate success of the therapy. There may be a number of issues but, again, it's important to prioritise and get the couple to focus on the main issue. They may also wander from the main issue and start to give more information on other areas. Try not to limit them, but at the same time encourage them to vent in a controlled environment. Often this is the first time they will have felt able to really express their frustrations and feelings, so emotions can run high.

The task for the therapist here is to capture the key issues for both adults within the couple. Their goals may well be the same but may differ. They may also be contradictory – for example, the stepparent may want to see less of their stepchild, whereas the biological parent may wish their child visited more frequently or resided on a permanent basis. While this can appear an almost irresolvable conflict, the focus of further therapeutic work might be to understand the difficulties in the relationship between the stepparent and the stepchild, and simultaneously help the biological parent value the time they spend with their child and be realistic in their demands and expectations.

Stage 3: Solutions

Once the background information has been gathered and key issues identified, work should begin in helping the couple deal more effectively with the presenting problems. The IST aims to focus on the specific issues the couple are presenting. As described earlier in the chapter, the assumption is that the couple have a fundamentally solid and normal relationship. The difficulties they are experiencing currently are related to stepfamily functioning and, if they are given the appropriate support and guidance, they will be able to continue developing their family independent of further external help.

Consequently, the focus of each session is very much on the issues the couple have brought to the session. These may well be related to other issues within the family or impact other relationships, however this should be evident as the sessions develop.

As each couple will bring different challenges, each needing different approaches, I have provided a number of case studies that serve to illustrate how therapists might begin to address specific issues. I have chosen families who were experiencing very different, but well-recognised, stepfamily issues. These are all presented in Chapter 7.

Toolkit 4.1 Helping family integration – 'playing the joker'

An exercise that can help stepfamilies integrate.

Toolkit 4.2 Family texting game

A light-hearted way of helping stepfamily members get to know one another better.

Further tools have been developed to use either in couple therapy or with groups. These can be found at the end of Chapter 5 and include the following.

Toolkit 5.1 Stepfamily quiz

A quiz to explore and learn about stepfamily dynamics and behaviour.

Toolkit 5.2 Shared expectations

An exercise to help members of a couple understand their own and their partner's expectations. Useful for initiating discussions and creating shared goals between the individuals.

Toolkit 5.3 Showing empathy

An exercise to help couples become more empathetic to their stepchildren's experiences within the stepfamily.

Toolkit 5.4 Couple strengths

An exercise to help couples evaluate the strength of their relationship, and identify areas for more focus and work.

Toolkit 5.5 Family health check

A questionnaire to help couples identify the strengths and weaknesses in their family.

Stage 4: Homework

The final stage of the model refers back to the core principles; this assumes the couple are the ones who are the instigators of change. It is therefore important that they view the sessions as ways of identifying the changes that are needed in their family, but recognise that the mechanisms for change are firmly within their own control. Often I ask couples to try things we have suggested in the session, or perhaps read material that I provide or direct them to.

Conclusion and key learning points

This chapter is at the heart of integrated support for stepfamilies and defines the counselling approach for couples. The model is based on the assumption that couples who seek support are struggling to deal with issues that are largely related to stepfamily functioning. Therefore if they are given the targeted support they need, they are likely to be able to move on in their relationships. Consequently the counselling is targeted at delivering solutions to couples that they can then apply in their own family units.

The interventions are broadly based around normalising the experiences of couples. Many couples approach counselling feeling that they are unique in their feelings and behaviour within the family. Recognising that their experiences are normal and expected allows them to deal more openly with the issues. Often couples will begin new relationships with unrealistic expectations about stepfamily life. One of the first tasks of the professional is to help the couple reassess their expectations, and make these more manageable and achievable. If the stepfamily is to survive and thrive, it is essential that the couple are strong enough to cope with the demands. As such the counsellor needs to equip them with the skills they need to be able to deal with the common issues that stepfamilies face and ensure they can communicate effectively.

Research has shown that two of the key areas where conflict is likely to arise are within the definition of the roles that stepparents assume and in the interactions between ex partners. A key part to play for therapists is, then, in helping couples clearly define their roles, understanding the benefits and issues with different types of role and, second, in setting clear boundaries with ex partners.

IST is a simple model based on a series of stages – from assessment through to identifying the key issues and setting clear goals for the family. The aim is to provide a 'light touch' for families, giving them tools that they can use to help develop their own families. The therapist should be there to guide them through the development process but should not become an integral part of the development. It should therefore be a process that is facilitated rather than directed by the counselling sessions.

Toolkit

This toolkit contains exercises that have been designed to support relationship professionals in their work with stepfamilies.

4.1   Helping family integration – 'playing the joker'

If couples are finding it difficult to integrate their family – for example, the stepparent may be feeling excluded from the biological unit, or the relationship between the stepparent and stepchildren is weak – it might be useful to suggest the following exercise to them.

This exercise can be used at weekends or in holiday periods, and is a good way of making all members of the stepfamily feel included. Each family member is given a 'joker' card – this can be real or imaginary, depending on the age of the children. Everyone is then entitled to 'play their joker' on an activity that they want everyone to get involved in. So, for example, during a holiday, this ensures that every family member gets to do something they want – and they can include the rest of the family. So, regardless of age, everyone feels they are being listened to.

All families find it hard to make time for everyone, but this can be even harder in stepfamilies, where children can have a wide range of ages. By using this system you can ensure that everyone has a chance to do something that they want to – and, more importantly, the rest of the family have to accept and enjoy the experience without complaint! I find this is useful for children and adults alike. While it works well on holidays, it can also be used to plan weekends. While it might not be possible for everyone to play their joker in a weekend, the adults can make their own rules that work for them, perhaps limiting it to one activity per week-end. Obviously it is also up to the couple to set boundaries such as costs – it might be that they can have a set budget or even identify only free activities.

4.2   Family texting game

This game can be a really good way to get to know one another better. The idea is to bring out fresh sides and new information about other members of the family. It is important to be positive and playful in this exercise – it's not an opportunity to be mean about other people! So, text other members of your family and ask them to complete the following statements. When these run out, think of some new ones of your own.

- If you were a superhero, you'd be …
- If you were a chocolate from the Black Magic box, you'd be …
- If you were a car, you'd be a …
- If you were a bird, you'd be a …
- If you were an animal, you'd be a …
- Your perfect job would be …
- Your perfect evening would be …
- Your perfect music track would be …
- If you were a flower, you'd be a …

This can be a good exercise to give to stepfamilies to try between sessions.

5 PSYCHO-EDUCATION AND BEHAVIOURAL MODELLING

Research has clearly identified that couples that are on second or multiple remarriages or relationships are more likely to divorce or separate (e.g. Booth and Edwards, 1992; Tzeng and Mare, 1995). Interestingly, however, these couples are not less satisfied with their relationships than first couples, with research consistently showing no significant difference between couples in terms of marital or relationship satisfaction. The difference appears to be related to couples that have children from prior relationships. Tzeng and Mare (1995) found that couples with children from prior relationships were 50 per cent more likely to divorce or separate from their partner. Given that the majority of children in stepfamilies live predominantly with their biological mother (Kreider and Fields, 2005), this may explain the higher divorce rate in stepfamilies.

Couples in stepfamilies are therefore at a greater risk of separating than couples with only biological children in their family. The need for effective early intervention is both highly relevant and, one might posit, key to increasing stepfamily stability (Halford *et al.*, 2003). Common problems are generally related to three distinct areas, as follows.

1. Couple relationship factors – including couple communication, their commitment to marriage and stepfamily expectations.
2. Parenting and child-related factors – agreement on child rearing, the relationship between the biological parent and child, and the relationship between the stepparent and stepchild.
3. External factors – Relationship with former partners and social support.

These areas therefore represent the target for interventions for step-families.

In order to be effective, interventions should be directed at prevention rather than treatment, targeting couples early on in their new relation-ships. Visher and Visher (1979) believed that most stepfamilies need education rather than therapy. Education about normal stepfamily development and stages would in this way better prepare stepfamily members and provide more realistic expectations (Papernow, 1984).

While offering traditional therapy or coaching for couples in crisis or struggling to cope with the demands of stepfamily life is clearly an effective approach, the need for broader, educational-based early inter-ventions should also be considered for stepfamilies. Given the evidence presented, it is suggested that this might reduce more critical therapeu-tic needs later in the relationships. This chapter considers the evidence for group-based psycho-educational programmes and offers research-based suggestions for programme content.

It addresses the following questions.

- What are the benefits of group education for stepfamilies?
- What is the evidence for efficacy for such programmes?
- What are the theoretical underpinnings of such interventions?
- What are the key elements of design and content when considering group education for stepfamilies?
- How are these programmes best delivered to stepfamilies?

Background

In a review of the literature, Adler-Baeder and Higginbotham (2004) argue that couples in stepfamilies could represent a significant propor-tion of the population served by relationship professionals. Visher and Visher (1996) found education to be the highest need for stepfamilies, suggesting that many couples would not reach the level of clinical need if education on stepfamily dynamics and development were provided preventatively. Evidence suggests that couples in stepfamilies might be at a greater risk of their relationships failing, however there is empiri-cal evidence that successful, well-adjusted stepfamilies can provide as nurturing an environment for all family members as well-adjusted biological families. Well-functioning and mature stepfamilies can also reduce the risks for poor child outcomes associated with divorce (Bray and Kelly, 1998; Hetherington and Kelly, 2002). Adler-Baeder and Higginbotham (2004) suggest that relationship professionals can therefore provide a valuable service to couples forming stepfamilies by distinguishing them from biological families and offering relationship programmes that specifically address their unique needs.

The benefits of psycho-education for stepfamilies

Researchers have identified many aspects of stepfamily living that have been enhanced through engagement in psycho-education or stepfamily-focused courses and workshops. It is worth noting that, in couples who choose to attend stepfamily or stepparenting courses, it is more often than not the woman (in mixed-sex couples) who initiates the sessions. Their partners, while happy to attend, are not generally the ones to identify the need or take action in finding a solution.

The areas where improvements have been identified are described in the following section. A pictorial representation of the short- and longer-term outcomes from an education programme is provided in Figure 5.1.

Meeting other stepfamilies

One of the issues for stepparents and stepfamilies in general is their level of isolation from biological families, and their inability to share and discuss issues with friends and wider family. Couples from stepfamilies often feel that friends don't really understand the pressures they face. Without having social norms or role models, couples often believe that their experiences are different from those of others and their problems unique. Once they are able to meet other couples in situations similar to their own, they can find a sense of relief that their experiences and feelings are shared by other stepfamilies. Skogrand, Davis and Higginbotham (2011) found that participants in their study spoke of no longer feeling alone, with other couples experiencing similar problems and feelings. This benefit was shared not only by the adults but also the children in the stepfamily. Couples can also learn from other couples, rather than just the course facilitator.

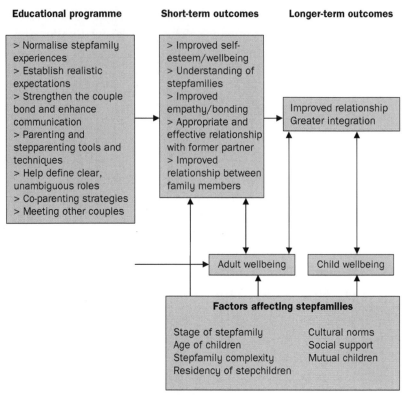

Figure 5.1 Factors related to psycho-education programme efficacy

Family bonding

In a study of stepfathers who attended a course with their partner (Higginbotham *et al.*, 2012), the majority of participants felt their family had benefited from improved family bonding. In particular they spoke of a stronger bond developing between themselves and their partner, together with better interaction with all family members. Other participants believed that a course involving all family members allowed them time to bond and get to know one another more (Skogrand *et al.*, 2011). They also recognised the importance of spending one-to-one time with each of the family members and together as a family (Higginbotham *et al.*, 2010).

Improved empathy

Participants in the Higginbotham, Skogrand and Torres (2010) study also expressed a greater awareness of their feelings for their stepchildren and the stresses they were experiencing, thus they were able to effectively 'stand in their shoes' and understand the difficulties from their stepchildren's perspective. Stepparent and stepchildren are therefore able to understand one another just that bit better, acknowledging that other family members may have differing views that lead to different behaviours and outcomes.

A more subtle effect of this form of education is in enabling the adults to empathise with their children and realise the importance of their ongoing relationship with their other biological parent. Once parents realise that their children feel guilty for loving both parents or having a good time with their other parent, they often make an effort to change the way they respond to their children, making it easier for them to talk about their absent biological parent positively, and encouraging visits and interaction (Higginbotham *et al.*, 2010). It is therefore a valuable skill to transfer to stepfamilies where complex and multiple relationships often lead to difficulties in the family development.

Improved communication

There is significant evidence (e.g. Skogrand *et al.*, 2011; Higginbotham *et al.*, 2012), to suggest that attending such a course will improve communication between family members. Participants felt that they had learned through their attendance at the course to communicate with their spouse and children more effectively. Many spoke of making the time to sit down and chat with both their partner and stepchildren on a regular basis and of making use of new communication techniques they had learned through the course. The improved communication also served to enhance their joint parenting skills and encouraged them to make joint decisions about the children.

Creating new family traditions

Individuals bring their own traditions and history into a stepfamily. While some of these traditions can be incorporated into the new family unit, it is important to help couples realise the benefit of creating their own set of traditions, which are unique to the family. These traditions help to define and develop the new family unit. Research has shown that education for couples can help them understand the benefits to be gained by developing family traditions and begin to put their individual stamp on their own family (Skogrand *et al.*, 2011).

Parenting skills

Many stepfathers from the same study (Higginbotham *et al.*, 2012) also commented on how attending the course had improved their parenting skills. These ranged from skills in terms of effective discipline methods – in particular, how to co-manage discipline with their partner – to simply having more patience in dealing with their stepchildren. This knowledge was particularly beneficial to men who had no prior experiencing of parenting. Further research has found evidence that couples experience perceived benefits in their relationship as a consequence of improved parenting (Bullard *et al.*, 2010).

Interacting with ex partners

Courses can also be useful in setting expectations around the relationship with ex partners. Clearly one of the biggest differences between stepfamilies and biological families is the need to maintain contact and co-parent with a previous partner. This can cause significant issues within the stepfamily, with new partners feeling isolated from discussions between the biological parents and old emotional ties difficult to deal with. Enabling discussion in group sessions can help individuals learn to cope more effectively with their ex partners, focusing on the practical issues rather than being led by emotion (Skogrand *et al.*, 2011).

Summary

It is clear that there are a broad number of potential benefits arising from psycho-education. However, it is less clear whether the benefits can be maintained by the family after the period of education has finished. Unfortunately, longitudinal research has yet to be carried out. What is evident, though, is that couples and stepfamilies in general benefit from psycho-education as an effective intervention to assist in the development of their new families. While the intervention can occur at any point in the stepfamily's development, research has suggested that early intervention is likely to be more effective in assisting the family members to develop an integrated stepfamily. The education also provides a protective factor as the family evolves and develops, with individuals drawing on the enhanced skills and knowledge gained from the programme. Finally, if professionals are able to provide this level of support for new stepfamilies, there is evidence that these stepfamilies will be less likely to need more clinical support at a later stage (Visher and Visher, 1996).

Theoretical approaches

A number of theoretical approaches have been considered in support of the need and direction of stepfamily psycho-education. These are discussed below.

Family systems theory

White and Klein (2008) defined a system as 'a unit that can be distinguished from and that affects the environment' (p.124). In the application to stepfamilies, the family unit can be considered a system that consists of various subsystems, including the stepfather, stepmother, stepchild, biological child and ex partner. Each subsystem is then linked with another with multiple interactions, creating complicated connections that are easily disturbed, pulling the family away from a state of equilibrium (Ingoldsby, Smith and Miller, 2004).

In order to help a stepfamily it is therefore essential for the relationship professional to address the family's pattern of interactions and relationships. Systems theory focuses on the process of problem solving rather than on the problem itself (Ingoldsby *et al.*, 2004). As the family grows and develops so the challenges change and evolve. Psycho-education offers the opportunity to enhance a couple's ability to solve complex problems and resolve conflict, leading to a healthier pattern of interaction and family development. The skills learned by couples therefore help them make sense of the complexity of their family structure and deal more effectively with the unique challenges they continue to face.

Behaviour Modeling Training

Behaviour Modeling Training (BMT) has become one of the most widely used and well-researched psychologically based training interventions. The approach is based on Bandura's Social Learning Theory (1977) and emphasises four component processes, namely attention, retention, reproduction and motivation.

Attentional processes are concerned with the individual observing modelling stimuli – for example, watching someone else carry out the desired skills or behaviour. The extent to which a person adheres to the modelled behaviour is influenced by a number of criteria including the characteristics of how the modelled behaviours are displayed (e.g. presented in increasing difficulty or complexity), the characteristics of the behaviours modelled (e.g. how distinctively they are presented), characteristics of the model (e.g. the perception of the modeller's expertise, and similarities between the individual learning and the model in terms of sex, race or age, and finally the characteristics of the individual learning (e.g. their capabilities and motivation) (Decker and Nathan, 1985).

Attentional processes are related to the transfer of the observed stimuli to short-term memory, whereas retentional processes are necessary for learning to transfer to long-term memory. These processes involve symbolic coding, where individuals organise behaviours presented during modelling into symbols that facilitate storage and retrieval at a later date (Decker and Nathan, 1985). In BMT, retentional processes can be invoked through the use of a learning style that facilitates symbolic coding and symbolic rehearsal (i.e. mental practice), encouraging the individual to rehearse how they plan to use the behaviours in practice.

Reproduction and motivational processes occur in BMT as individuals practise the skills demonstrated through modelling and apply them in real-life situations. Practice during BMT, referred to as behavioural rehearsal or skill practice, includes feedback from other trainees or participants and the facilitator. This feedback loop serves not only a correctional function but also offers motivation through social reinforcement (i.e. praise) when participants demonstrate the new skills effectively.

BMT differs from other training approaches in its prescriptive use of the following elements:

- describing to participants a set of well-defined behaviours/skills
- providing a model displaying the effective use of the behaviours
- providing opportunities to practise the behaviours
- providing feedback and social reinforcement to participants
- taking steps to maximise the transfer of the behaviours.

While other approaches often include individual or several components from the above list, BMT emphasises the importance of including all elements.

This approach was used as the basis for a web-based, interactive and self-administered stepfamily psycho-educational programme (Gelatt, Adler-Baeder and Seeley, 2010). The programme relies heavily on visual demonstrations of behaviours related to couple, parenting and stepparenting practices, and helps to promote knowledge acquisition and improvement in attitudes, intentions and self-efficacy. The findings from this programme suggested that participation in the stepfamily education programme positively influenced several key areas of parenting and family functioning, including role adjustment, harmony, life satisfaction, parent–child conflict, learning not to 'overreact' to situations, and positive parenting intentions.

Behavioural family intervention

Some researchers in the field (e.g. Higginbotham *et al.*, 2010) advocate the benefits of including children, rather than just the adults, in education programmes. They point to the field of behavioural parent training, or behavioural family intervention (Sanders, Gooley and Nicholson, 2000), which suggests that children are influenced when parents' behaviours and parent–child interactions are modified (Nicholson and Sanders, 1999). While the initial application of this framework has related to children with severe behavioural problems, there is a growing body of evidence to support the efficacy of the intervention for children with difficulties related to stepfamily living (Nicholson and Sanders, 1999).

However, it could be argued that children can still benefit from the education their parents and stepparents participate in, even if they themselves don't attend. Assuming the programme offers support and skills enhancement in modifying the parent's or stepparent's behaviour, the theory suggests that children's behaviour would be affected accordingly.

Summary

The above theories have all been applied to various stepparenting programmes, with clear benefits to the families participating. The underlying theories suggest that, in order to be effective, programmes should consider a number of key factors. These are summarised below.

- Stepparenting programmes should provide clear guidance for stepfamily members in terms of coping more effectively with stepfamily-related issues.

- It is important to consider membership of the workshops. There are benefits to including both the adults and the children, however this may not always be feasible or practical. It is essential, however, that both adults attend any such course or training.
- At the beginning of the course, it is important to find out from the participants the state of all relationships in the family. Often this can be achieved by asking them to consider this on a worksheet. This offers a good opportunity to get them to reflect on both the positive and negative aspects of each relationship.
- Workshops should focus on giving the participants lots of support in terms of addressing their specific issues. Often this can be achieved by asking them to identify their objectives in coming to the course. A good facilitator will ensure that these are addressed throughout the course.
- There should be opportunities within the workshops for couples to be given examples of the desired behaviours modelled and for them to practise these in a safe environment.
- Make the course fun! For example, provide prizes when teams or couples get things right. Consider using quizzes or other interactive sessions to ensure that the participants understand the material being presented.

Themes and topics

The core topics around which a programme should be created and designed are those identified in Chapter 3. These include normalising the stepfamily experience, establishing realistic expectations, strengthening the couple bond and communication, developing clear, unambiguous stepparent roles and setting clear boundaries for communicating with ex partners. A review of existing programmes, targeted at stepfamilies, reveals a similar range of approaches and content (see Adler-Baeder and Higginbotham, 2004). These are discussed below, together with suggestions for content.

Normalising the stepfamily

It is almost 40 years since Cherlin (1978) first made his observation about stepfamilies being regarded as an incomplete institution, and it could be argued that little has really changed. Stepfamilies still often feel stigmatised in society and have few role models to aspire to or even to help clarify their own role in the new family unit. For example, in the UK stepparents have no legal rights towards their stepchildren unless they go through a formal adoption process, which is particularly unlikely if both biological parents are still alive and involved with their children. Socially, the role of stepparents remains confusing. Should they be involved in schooling decisions for their stepchildren? Should they take an active role in disciplining their stepchildren? Should they been encouraged to attend school functions such as parents evenings or sports days? Without clear guidelines, stepparents often feel confused, frustrated and isolated. The ongoing involvement of ex partners often leads to anger on the part of the stepparent at their inability to control their 'own world'. Wider family and friends are often unable to provide adequate support, not quite understanding the issues that the family are having to cope with.

This is one of the cornerstones of any education programme and is easily covered within a group setting. The simple act of meeting others in the same situation helps couples realise that their behaviours and feelings are normal and to be expected. It is recommended therefore that facilitators have explicit discussions with couples and provide information that validates their experiences. This may include discussing social stigma, lack of clear role models, lack of social support and the legal ambiguity of their relationship, despite potentially being a primary carer for their stepchildren. Validation provided in this way has frequently been found to be helpful to couples (e.g. Visher, Visher and Pasley, 2003). The group setting facilitates these discussions, and allows couples to share their experiences and feelings.

> **Toolkit 5.1 Stepfamily quiz**
>
> *A quiz to explore and learn about stepfamily dynamics and behaviour.*

Realistic expectations

Research suggests that, if couples have realistic expectations about stepfamily dynamics, and the time required to develop and integrate the family unit and establish clear roles and responsibilities, they are more likely to thrive and survive (e.g. Hetherington and Kelly, 2002; Visher *et al.*, 2003). Expectations of 'instant love' between stepparents and stepchildren are clearly unrealistic, as is the expectation that all family members will adjust to the new stepfamily easily and quickly. Couples who hold these expectations frequently experience lower satisfaction in their relationship (Hetherington and Kelly, 2002).

There is consistent evidence that, for both clinical and non-clinical samples, the first few years together can be turbulent (e.g. Bray and Kelly, 1998), with relationships at greater risk of failing in the first five years (Clarke and Wilson, 1994) The first two years, while often being referred to as a 'honeymoon period', are frequently disorganised and turbulent, with couples trying to make sense of what is often a very complex situation. Their expectations rarely match the reality, and this can lead to arguments and disagreements between the couple and other family members. It is only when they are able to address these issues, and set out the rules and roles that are appropriate for their family, that they are able to move on to a period of stabilisation (e.g. Hetherington and Kelly, 2002).

There are no prescribed roles for stepparents, however there is evidence to suggest that couples who are able to define and agree on roles and rules within their own family are more likely to be successful and move faster through the process of family integration (e.g. Bray and Kelly, 1998). Stepfamilies who take their time to form and build relationships slowly are more likely to succeed than those who force and push for integration. The aim is to facilitate an environment of mutual respect and trust, and use this as the basis on which to build the new family unit.

In order to address these common issues, an education programme should help participants understand the barriers to development and be encouraged to develop healthy expectations. By sharing the fact that most stepfamilies take at least four years to develop, stepfamilies at an early point in their relationship can allow themselves more time and space. Often it can come as a relief for couples when they realise they are doing as well as they should be. Sharing with participants the stepfamily cycle (Papernow, 1993) is often useful as they can identify with the stages and work out the barriers for progression. In agreeing roles and rules, couples will have to display empathy with their partner, and use mature negotiating and communication skills. These are all useful components of an education programme, as we know from research that these traits are often present in well-functioning stepfamilies (Visher and Visher, 1996). Finally, sharing knowledge about possible roles for stepparents can also be valuable, rather than letting them simply define their own role. Participants can then understand the benefits and known difficulties with adopting different roles within the family, and can adapt these to their own family circumstances. Some examples of this are provided at the end of the chapter.

In a developmental approach to stepfamilies, Papernow (2013) has identified several stages of normal stepfamily development, which follow one another chronologically (see Table 5.1). Progression from one stage to the next depends upon a degree of success in meeting the challenges of the previous stage. The first stages (fantasy, immersion) form a group referred to as the 'early stages'. This is the time when the family begins to form, and is characterised by the aspirations of the family members for their new beginning and the formation of a new family unit, setting new boundaries and expectations. The 'middle stages', consisting of 'mobilisation' and 'action', describes a phase of restructuring within the family to accommodate the changes felt in the early stages, usually as the stepparent presses for change in order to become a more equal partner and member of the family. It is often during this phase that couples seek the support and advice of professionals. The 'later stages', however, are characterised by greater intimacy, and are where all family members feel accepted and part of the new family unit. Families vary widely in the length of time they take to progress through the cycle, but Papernow (2013) points out that no family she studied took less than four years. Moreover, seven years was the average period of time for progression and some families remained trapped in the early stages after as long as twelve years, with divorce resulting in a number of families that had failed to progress.

Table 5.1 Stepfamily development stages (Papernow, 2013)

Stage 1	Fantasy – the honeymoon period, filled with unrealistic expectations
Stage 2	Immersion – unmet expectations, disappointment and differences
Stage 3	Mobilisation – a new beginning; couples begin to discuss the issues
Stage 4	Action – working together to make the changes necessary
Stage 5	Contact – a sense of intimacy and closeness starts to develop
Stage 6	Resolution – the development cycle is complete

The staged approach to stepfamily development is a useful tool for therapists and counsellors to consider when working with stepfamilies, both in helping them make sense of where the clients are in terms of their own development and in helping the couple understand the extent of their journey. While it can be difficult to explain the time it will take for them to develop, often this allows them to become more relaxed and satisfied with their progress. They are then free to work together to make the changes necessary to move through the stages with greater confidence.

Toolkit 5.2 Shared expectations

An exercise to help members of a couple understand their own and their partner's expectations. Useful for initiating discussions and creating shared goals between the individuals.

The stepparent–stepchild relationship

The relationship between the stepparent and stepchild is somewhat unique. This relationship is by definition the newest in the family, and is central to the ongoing success and development of the stepfamily. It is important to remember that neither the stepparent nor the stepchild has chosen the relationship, rather it has been foisted on them by the development of the couple relationship. Research (e.g. Bray and Kelly, 1998) informs us that the quality of the stepparent–stepchild relation-ship affects couple conflict and the couple relationship. For example, we know that stepparents who do not immediately take on the role of disciplinarian, but step back and take the lead from the biological par-ent, are more satisfied with their relationship with their stepchild (e.g. Bray and Kelly, 1998). The age of the child is also of relevance, with younger children (less than 9 years of age) being more accepting of a stepparent than older children. Adolescent and pre-adolescent children, for example, often initiate conflict with stepparents (Hetherington and Kelly, 2002).

It is helpful here to provide strategies for the stepparent in helping them build stronger relationships with their stepchildren. Allowing time for the relationship to develop, showing mutual trust and respect before attempting to discipline, employing empathy to understand what it might be like to be in the stepchild's position, and adjusting their behaviour depending on the age and gender of the child, are all topics to introduce and discuss. It may also be useful to provide information on child development and behavioural management techniques, particularly for adults who are not biological parents. Finally, setting realistic expectations with regard to this relationship would also be beneficial. Research has suggested that stepparents do not have to achieve the same level of parent–child bond common in biological families in order to be successful in their role (Hetherington and Kelly, 2002).

> ### Toolkit 5.3 Showing empathy
>
> *An exercise to help couples become more empathetic to their stepchildren's experiences within the stepfamily.*

Building the couple relationship

Unlike in biological families, the couple relationship is pre-dated by relationships between the parent and child. This makes the relationship vulnerable to demands placed on individuals from other relationships within the family unit. Family theory informs us that one relationship can and will have ripple effects on the interrelated relationships. Parents, for example, are often protective of their biological children within a new stepfamily. This can leave the stepparent feeling isolated and place additional strains on the couple relationship, where there are competing needs on time and emotions. It is therefore essential that the couple give priority to strengthening and developing their relationship, in order to be able to deal appropriately and fairly with the children in the family. There is evidence from both clinical and non-clinical samples that, if couples make time to put their relationship first, stress in the family will be reduced (Dahl, Cowgill and Asmundsson, 1987; Visher *et al.*, 2003).

A key aspect of any education programme for stepfamilies must consider the couple relationship. Participants need to understand that their relationship is vulnerable and fragile, and therefore needs attention, particularly early on in the relationship. Activities that help strengthen their relationship should be encouraged (e.g. improved communication, resolving conflict, empathy for each other's situation).

> **Toolkit 5.4 Couple strengths**
>
> *An exercise to help couples evaluate the strength of their relationship, and identify areas for more focus and work.*

Relationships with ex partners

Stepfamilies are not a new phenomenon, however it is only more recently, with the rise in divorce and separation, that couples have found themselves having to navigate relationships both within their immediate families and with former partners who remain involved with their children. There is significant evidence to suggest that both acrimonious and ongoing relationships with former spouses can negatively impact the new couple's partnership (e.g. Buunk and Mutsaers, 1999; Knox and Zusman, 2001). It is essential that individuals manage to emotionally separate from their ex partners and set appropriate boundaries with their former spouse if they are to develop and maintain a healthy relationship with their new partner (Weston and Macklin, 1990). It is also known that children's behaviour is affected by the relationship between their parents. Thus if there is ongoing conflict between the parents, the children's behaviour is likely to be negatively impacted (Amato, 2000). The ongoing influence of an ex on a stepfamily can also lead to more stress being experienced by both the stepparent and the biological parent, which in turn can affect all the relationships in the stepfamily. The children pick up on the conflict, even if it is unspoken, and can become anxious and worried when the adults have to communicate and interact. They may also start to experience loyalty conflicts, drawing back from engaging with stepparents for fear that the absent biological parent will be further upset.

Education programmes should consider helping couples understand the different types of co-parenting that are available, together with the benefits and risks of these approaches. Skills in learning how to manage these relationships and put in place clear boundaries should be also be included. The main emphasis is on developing a business-like, respectful relationship with ex partners. Finally, it important to stress to couples that, by improving these relationships, they are likely to reduce the stress within their own relationship.

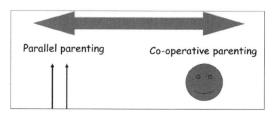

Figure 5.2 Example of a scale, with parallel parenting at one extreme and co-operative parenting at the other

Individuals 'co-parent' with their former partner in different ways and for different reasons. If the separation or divorce has been amicable it may be relatively easy to communicate, however if the split was associated with a lot of animosity, working together may be fraught with difficulties.

I suggest that counsellors and therapists introduce the concept of a 'scale' (like the one in Figure 5.2) with co-operative parenting at one extreme and working completely independently, or in parallel, at the other. However, it is important to recognise that most co-parents move up and down the scale over time. There may be times when direct communication is going well, however something occurs that initiates conflict (such as a new partner) and attempts to communicate repeatedly fail. In these circumstances parents should consciously consider moving down the continuum towards parallel parenting, perhaps using written communication or a mediator until things improve.

Co-parenting relationships work best if the parents are business-like and courteous to each other, rather than emotionally involved. This is critical for new relationships and marriages as they are often negatively affected when previous partners are too attached and engaged with each other. Boundaries for the new couple relationship are therefore really important.

Parallel parenting

Most parents have to resort to this type of co-parenting at some point in their relationship. Typical behaviours include:

- little or no face-to-face or direct contact
- everything in writing
- neutral locations
- limit communication to essential facts.

This type of co-parenting is by its nature very distant. Both parents continue parenting their child or children but with little communication between them. Everything tends to be quite formal, with communication limited to email or text. Conversations tend to be rare, usually because in the past these have escalated into greater conflict. The children tend to have possessions at both homes or, alternatively, one parent takes on the responsibility of providing everything for their child. The parents are generally frightened to move from this position as they worry about greater conflict, however often this position softens over time. This is an appropriate style of co-parenting when the relationship is still conflictual, however it is important that children aren't forced to act as messengers between the warring parents.

Co-operative parenting

This is much more of a shared experience, where both parents are able to communicate effectively in discussions related to their joint children. However, it is often difficult for couples to achieve this, particularly when a divorce or split is still relatively recent. For parents who are struggling to achieve this and are desperate to have a less conflictual relationship, the following advice is recommended.

- Let the children know that it's OK for them to talk about their other parent or to get in touch with them. Suggest that they get in touch – for example, 'Would you like to let your dad know that you came top in the maths test?' is a really good way to let your child know that it's OK to talk to their other parent. They then don't have to worry about what you might think or say.
- Acknowledge and encourage the child's need for a relationship with the other biological parent.
- Find something you respect about your ex and say it.
- Use non-judgemental, neutral language when talking about the other biological parent.
- Make allowances for different parenting styles – their way (or yours!) is not the only way.
- Find solutions and compromises – don't try to win.
- Know when to call for a break and move to parallel parenting.
- Be flexible – co-parenting is rarely straightforward and plans may have to change occasionally.
- Put things in writing if there is confusion.

Remind clients that, when couples separate, both parents have their children for less time so there will always be occasions when things don't work out the way they want them to and they will have to compromise. For example, everyone wants to have their children with them on special occasions such as Christmas and birthdays, but both parents need to share the time and compromise.

If there are ongoing issues related to co-parenting, it is important that the therapist clarify the current situation. The following questions, together with the explanation above on the co-parenting scale, should facilitate this.

- What types of co-parenting occur in the stepfamily?
- Where do they consider they sit on the co-parenting scale (parallel or co-operative parenting)? Has that changed recently?
- Are they happy with the relationship?
- What would they like to change?

Toolkit 5.5 Family health check

An exercise to help families work out their strengths and areas that need attention.

Programme design considerations

There are clearly many ways of designing and approaching the design of stepfamily education training, however the following points have been drawn from existing literature, with evidence of improved efficacy.

It is recommended that programmes include and refer to appropriate research, and employ a theoretical framework wherever possible. This provides a strong foundation on which to build the course components. Employing a variety of teaching methods that promote participant interaction is always preferable to using a didactic approach. By engaging in discussions and activities, couples are more likely to retain the information and be more capable of making the behavioural changes required to improve the dynamics in their families. In support of this, facilitators are encouraged to use a broad selection of tools and media. Some examples are provided at the end of this chapter. Finally, as with all training programmes, participant feedback should always be gathered to provide ongoing enhancement and improvement of the course and materials.

Delivery methods

This chapter has presented evidence of a number of significant benefits that can be realised through the delivery of psycho-education for stepfamilies. However, it is worth considering the potential delivery methods of these programmes. While the obvious approach would be a group format and face to face, this might not be feasible or favoured for many couples. The following sections discuss some of the alternative approaches for the delivery of educational support to stepfamilies.

Online support

Research for the United States has produced evidence that both online support groups (Christian, 2005) and self-help group meetings (Jones, 2004) are effective at providing support to stepmothers, as they allow them to vent their frustration without fear of perpetuating the negative stereotypes that accompany their role, and provide them with support to effect positive changes in their families. However, one of the potential issues with this approach is that the meetings or online groups will serve to reinforce and focus on the issues rather than the solutions or coping mechanisms. It is therefore recommended that these approaches are facilitator led or moderated (for online groups), to encourage sharing of experiences and solutions rather than dwelling on the difficulties and issues.

Group-facilitated workshops

While the primary aims of existing parenting programmes are predominantly to increase parental confidence and skills in communicating with and managing a child's behaviour, the primary aims of a stepparenting programme, as discussed earlier, do not need to be as closely aligned with the parenting role, but rather should focus on helping stepfamilies recognise 'normal' stepfamily development and functioning, and enhance their ability to negotiate co-parenting relationships (Adler-Baeder, 2001).

In North America, there are a number of intervention programmes designed specifically for stepfamilies. A review of stepfamily curricula by Adler-Baeder and Higginbotham (2004) identified eight such programmes. Many of these, however, have subsequently been criticised for their methodological problems and lack of an empirical basis (Whitton *et al.*, 2008). The review by Adler-Baeder *et al.* (2004) suggested that, while many of the programmes use empirical references, only two offer documentation of empirically validated programme effects and evaluation instruments: 'Stepping Stones' (Olsen, 1997) and 'Smart Steps for Adults and Children in Stepfamilies' (Adler-Baeder, 2001). Stepping Stones is a six-hour programme designed for home study or provision through facilitated groups (Adler-Baeder and Higginbotham, 2004), but is not based on any recognised theoretical framework. The programme has been evaluated to measure any increase in participants' knowledge on stepparenting, but the results remain unpublished. Smart Steps is a 12-hour programme developed by Adler-Baeder (2001) and intended to be delivered through facilitated groups. It is based on an ecological family systems framework. Adler-Baeder *et al.* (2004) argue that the programme helps stepfamily members realise that they need to establish roles and rules that work for their family, and that the application of biological family rules and expectations is not appropriate. They further suggest that existing non-stepfamily parenting programmes generally do not focus on the relationship between the couple, however within stepfamilies this relationship is often negatively affected by other relationships within the family unit, such as those between the stepparent and stepchildren. As well as these 'intra-household' relationships, stepparenting programmes have a strong emphasis on managing the 'inter-household' relationships and helping stepfamilies cope with the difficulties that arise from the complicated relationships between former partners. Recent evidence from research on 200 participants has found the Smart Steps programme effective in improving healthy relationship skills, increasing commitment to the relationship and decreasing relationship instability (Higginbotham and Adler-Baeder, 2008).

In the UK, specific support for stepfamilies is minimal. There is no central government-funded or charity-based resource centre for stepfamilies, therefore support is somewhat fragmented and unstructured. There is a generic family online support centre delivered through www.familylives.org.uk, which offers support to all families, including stepfamilies. Support tends to concentrate on online support and online chat, with face-to-face and support groups available in some regional areas. However, there is no standard workshop or educational programme offered currently. A review of online support offered via independent counsellors and therapists suggests that some are targeting services towards stepfamilies, however while group support sessions are offered these adopt a solely therapeutic approach and tend to ignore psycho-educational components.

A psycho-educational programme is currently offered via www.happysteps.co.uk. This can be delivered in a group setting in a single day-long workshop, or over four weekly sessions. While there are no published results on the efficacy of the programme, results from a small sample suggest that the programme was effective in improving a number of factors, including a reduction in stepparent anxiety, an increase in confidence in stepparenting and an increase in stepfamily integration.

Toolkit 5.6 Stepfamily couples workshop

A suggested outline for a series of workshops that can be tailored for couples in stepfamilies.

Web-based programmes

Some research has suggested that self-administered parenting programmes may be as effective as facilitator-administered treatments (e.g. Nicholson and Sanders, 1999). A further report by the US Department of Education (2010), which conducted a meta-analysis and review of online learning studies, found that learning outcomes for adults who engaged in online learning exceeded those of adults who received face-to-face instruction. Gelatt *et al.* (2010) used this research as the basis for developing and evaluating an interactive web-based programme for stepfamilies.

The programme uses a behaviour modelling approach, with the use of videos to demonstrate effective couple, parenting and stepparenting behaviours. Users are presented with different stepfamily challenges, with video clips dramatising the difficulties experienced. The participants are expected to select their response to the challenge via different options, one of which will be the desired response, while the others represent ineffective responses. They are then encouraged to view all the options to understand the likely effects of each approach. Each challenge area is likely to take between 20 and 30 minutes, with participants able to work their way through all the challenges at their own pace. Results from the study suggest that participation in the programme positively influenced several key areas of parenting and family functioning, including adjustment to stepfamily life, life satisfaction, parent–child conflict and more positive parenting intentions (e.g. not overreacting to child behaviours).

Individual couple training

While psycho-education lends itself to a group approach, it is also possible to adopt a structured approach on a one-to-one basis. One such programme is the Oregon Model of Parent Management Training (PMTO) (Forgatch and DeGarmo, 1999), which is a 13-session programme delivered in an individual-family format. Each session includes prescribed content, role play and modelling exercises, and targets five core parenting practices: skill encouragement, discipline, monitoring, problem solving and positive involvement. This programme was originally developed as a generic parenting model but has been evaluated for stepparents. A study conducted by Bullard *et al.* (2010) on newly formed stepfamilies (less than two years together) suggested that the programme was effective at improving the couple relationship. It also had a positive impact on parenting and stepparenting practices, and these in turn were associated with fewer child externalising behaviour problems. In addition, the research also provided evidence to support the hypothesis that changes in one family domain can impact on other domains. The impact of changes in parenting practices, for example, has related impacts on the couple relationship. Similarly, child behaviour problems have a powerful effect on couple satisfaction. It appears that the improvement in use of core skills, delivered via the programme, impacts on different areas within the stepfamily.

Summary

There are clearly a number of approaches practitioners may wish to consider when providing psycho-education to stepfamilies, however there are a number of common threads through these programmes that are the key to success and improvements for clients. The information delivered within psycho-education is predominantly targeted at couples in the early stages of stepfamily development, with most of the programmes actively targeting couples who have been together for less than two years. It is during this time that couples are most receptive to advice and support in putting in place the foundations of the new family unit.

In terms of content, while there are differences between programmes and approaches, there are a number of core elements that should be covered. These include a clear understanding of common stepfamily issues, setting realistic expectations, normalising the stepfamily experience, enhancing couple communication, problem solving, clear definition of roles within the family, and parenting and stepparenting practices. Many face-to-face programmes also encourage the stepfamily to engage in 'homework' or further reading to extend and embed the new skills and knowledge.

Conclusion and key learning points

The provision of psycho-education and behaviour modelling techniques is an area that has yet to be fully explored in terms of delivery to stepfamilies. There are areas of development, particularly in North America and Australia, where programmes have been developed and delivered with cautious optimism. Also, there appear to be key benefits for couples in stepfamilies, specifically those who are relatively new to their roles. Anecdotal evidence from programmes in the UK suggests that couples find these types of programme beneficial in a number of ways. Clearly, the programmes help to inform them on common stepfamily issues and provide additional coping mechanisms, however – and almost more importantly – they provide an opportunity to meet with others in the same situation and normalise their experiences. Stepparents often feel isolated in their roles, feeling that no one really understands their position. In meeting with others they are able to relax and feel more confident in dealing with issues in a more ordered and timely way.

This introduces an interesting question: does it therefore matter what content is delivered within the programme? Should the main priority be in facilitating these groups, allowing couples in stepfamilies the opportunity to meet others in similar situations, and share problems and potential approaches, based on their own experiences? Given the lack of current practice in this field I think it's still too early to make firm judgements. What we do know through evidence and current work is that this type of approach has a place within therapy for stepfamilies. While this area continues to grow in terms of both demand from families and services offered by professionals, I urge practitioners to continue to explore the unique needs of stepfamilies and consider psycho-education and group-facilitated training. We know from extensive research that stepfamilies face a plethora of common issues, which they are often ill prepared to deal with. If they can find help from professionals to understand and cope more effectively with these, in a supportive and encouraging environment, they are more likely to survive and thrive, providing a more secure family unit for their children and stepchildren.

Toolkit

The following exercises and tools may be useful to professionals when delivering psycho-education, either in a group setting or to individual clients.

5.1 Stepfamily quiz

In a group setting, a light-hearted quiz is a great way of reinforcing key messages. It is often useful to use this after an initial presentation and introduction related to stepfamily dynamics and common issues. I suggest that there are two ways of running this type of exercise: either dividing the group into two 'teams' and setting up a competition between the two 'sides', or asking each participant to take part individually.

The team approach requires the facilitator to divide the group into teams, perhaps by gender. This splits up the couples and encourages bonding between the participants. If possible, provide each team with a bell or buzzer so that they can clearly signal their answer. For the individual approach, I ask all participants to stand up. If they agree with the statement then they should put their hands on their head, if they disagree, they should place their hands on their bottom. This is sometimes known as 'heads and tails'. When a person gets a question wrong they have to sit down, meaning the last person standing is the winner.

I find that this approach helps normalise their own experiences of being part of the stepfamily and begins to build relationships within the group. Facilitators can introduce a number of true/false statements as part of the quiz, based on common misconceptions and truths about stepfamilies. When the participant provides the correct answer, or one that reflects research findings, the facilitator should explain and provide more information before moving on to the next question. At the end of the quiz it's always a good icebreaker to give the winner or winning team a small prize – chocolates or sweets often go down well. Some examples of statements for use in the quiz are given below, however these are merely suggestions.

Suggested true/false statements for use in the quiz

- Attachment needs to happen quickly between stepparents and stepchildren.
- Younger children find it more difficult than older children to adapt to stepparents.
- It takes at least four years for a stepfamily to develop and integrate.
- Stepmothers find it harder than stepfathers to cope in stepfamilies.
- Part-time stepparenting is easier than full-time stepparenting.
- Stepparents should step back from disciplining their stepchildren at the beginning of the relationship.
- Couples in stepfamilies have poorer social support than biological couples.
- Stepparents shouldn't ask their stepchildren to help with chores when they come to stay.
- It is easier for stepparents if the absent parent has limited contact with their children.

A maximum of ten questions is recommended to ensure that the quiz does not last too long and take up too much time in the workshop or programme.

5.2   Shared expectations

The exercise presented in Table 5.2 helps the practitioner understand where the couple have shared expectations and where they might differ. She or he can then work with the couple on

Table 5.2   Shared expectations exercise

Do you agree with these statements?			
1	A family holiday should include all our children, including stepchildren	Y	N
2	I think stepparents should attend school events	Y	N
3	Children should always go to their biological parent first if they have a problem	Y	N
4	I expect my stepchildren to treat me in the same way as they treat their mother/father	Y	N
5	I treat my stepchildren as though they are my own	Y	N
6	It's my job as much as my partner's to look after my stepchildren when they are with us	Y	N
7	My partner should be responsible for disciplining her/his children	Y	N
8	Stepchildren want a stepparent's affection and support	Y	N
9	I expect my stepchildren to obey the rules I make in the household	Y	N
10	Frequent contact with an ex spouse over issues concerning the children is normal	Y	N
11	The new spouse should adopt the rules of the household that the children have been living in	Y	N
12	A parent doesn't have to put either their new partner or their children first – they can love them equally	Y	N
13	The new couple relationship automatically gives the stepparent both the responsibility and the authority to discipline their partner's children	Y	N
14	Children should have a say in house rules	Y	N
15	I'd rather people didn't know we are a stepfamily	Y	N
16	I resent my partner spending time with their children	Y	N
17	It's OK to expect young children to call a stepparent mummy or daddy, even if they don't want to	Y	N
18	All children should be encouraged to help around the house	Y	N

addressing the differences and finding compromise where possible. Both members of the stepfamily couple should complete a questionnaire and then compare answers afterwards, ideally with the practitioner. Some questions are relevant only if the individual has stepchildren, therefore they should be instructed to omit these if necessary.

5.3 Showing empathy

This exercise is best used when working with several couples in a group environment. Ask the couples to start discussing and writing down the kinds of problem that children in stepfamilies might experience. For example, they might struggle with having to share a bedroom with a stepsibling, or perhaps they might have different rules to stick to in their different homes. Let them have a couple of minutes on this exercise and then, quietly, go round to a few individuals and ask them to swap with others, mixing up the couples. Don't explain what you're doing and don't give them any further instruction other than to carry on the exercise.

After a few more minutes ask them to stop and, before discussing the lists they've created, ask them how they felt about being asked to move. Normally, they will have experienced confusion, frustration or even annoyance at being split up from their partner. This simple exercise helps the couples to understand what it might feel like to be a child being asked to move between parents' homes, and often having no real voice. While the exercise allows couples to experience these emotions, it also provides a good opportunity for further discussion around the needs of children in stepfamilies.

5.4 Couple strengths

The exercise presented in Table 5.3 is a good light-hearted one to use with couples to assess their relationship. It is not intended to be entirely measurable, however it should identify some possible issues in the couple relationship. This is something that can help initiate a session related to their relationship. The aim is to begin to probe problem areas, for example related to discipline or perhaps the perceived lack of shared values. It can be used as a take-home exercise or some of the questions can be raised within

Table 5.3 Relationship assessment exercise

Would you say these statements are true or false?		
1	T/F	My partner and I work together to resolve problems
2	T/F	My partner and I have similar views on discipline
3	T/F	I find it easy to raise problems about my stepchildren with my partner
4	T/F	I am very happy in my relationship with my partner
5	T/F	I know my partner's current major worries
6	T/F	I look forward to spending time with my partner
7	T/F	My partner is one of my best friends
8	T/F	I am genuinely interested in my partner's opinion
9	T/F	I feel we have an equal say when we make decisions
10	T/F	We try to keep a sense of humour
11	T/F	My partner and I are a good team
12	T/F	I accept there are issues that we can't resolve
13	T/F	We share similar views about our roles in the family
14	T/F	We can both admit when we are wrong
15	T/F	I can talk to my partner about anything

the session for further discussion. I tend to find it is preferable to allow couples to complete this on their own so that they are really honest about their feelings and behaviours.

Scoring

13 or more TRUE answers

Well done. You appear to have developed a really good working relationship with your partner. Keep up the good work. Focus on the areas that you didn't agree with, and try to understand why that might be and what you could do to change things for the better.

7 to 12 TRUE answers

While you have many strengths you can build on, there are also some weaknesses you need to address. Congratulate yourself on the areas where you have developed a positive relationship with your partner – and don't lose sight of this, but take a look at the areas where you could improve.

6 or fewer TRUE answers

You really need to take time to talk to your partner and start working on strengthening your relationship. You need to be honest with each other and make a concerted effort to build a closer, more caring relationship. Don't be disheartened – you can make the changes that matter if you really want to.

5.5 Family health check

The questionnaire presented in Table 5.4 is a useful one to use with the couple at the beginning of therapy or at the beginning of a workshop. It helps identify problem areas and also identifies their family strengths. This is particularly valuable as there are often positives in the family that go unnoticed due to ongoing issues. This allows the therapist to praise the couple and make sure they recognise the strengths they already have. Both adults in the couple need to complete the questionnaire independently and then be encouraged to share their responses and discuss them with the therapist or facilitator.

5.6 Stepfamily couples workshop

The following topics should be considered in any form of education provided to couples in stepfamilies. By adopting a modular approach, course facilitators can deliver these in a single day, or over a period of weeks, depending on the needs of participants.

Session 1: What is a stepfamily?

This session is around normalising the stepfamily/blended family and setting realistic expectations.

Table 5.4 Family strengths exercise

Rate your family strengths (strongly disagree = 1; strongly agree = 5)					
We are a happy family unit	1	2	3	4	5
We have realistic expectations	1	2	3	4	5
We are in agreement about roles and responsibilities	1	2	3	4	5
We have a strong couple relationship	1	2	3	4	5
There is generally good communication within and across households	1	2	3	4	5
We can rely on our family and friends for support	1	2	3	4	5
We try to be flexible to accommodate everyone	1	2	3	4	5
We include all the children in our family – whether they're with us all the time or part of the time	1	2	3	4	5
TOTAL					
Rate your relationship (needs a lot of work = 1; no issues = 5)					
Couple	1	2	3	4	5
My relationship with my ex	1	2	3	4	5
My partner's relationship with their ex	1	2	3	4	5
Parent–child 1	1	2	3	4	5
Parent–child 2	1	2	3	4	5
Parent–child 3	1	2	3	4	5
Stepparent–child 1	1	2	3	4	5
Stepparent–child 2	1	2	3	4	5
Stepparent–child 3	1	2	3	4	5
Stepsibling combinations	1	2	3	4	5
In-laws (mine)	1	2	3	4	5
In-laws (my partner's)	1	2	3	4	5

- Stepfamily statistics
- Myths and realities
- Realistic expectations
- Identify family strengths

Session 2: Developing roles and rules

A session designed to help clarify roles in stepfamilies and empower families to set boundaries and rules for their own family unit.

- The ambiguity of stepfamily roles
- Identifying different stepparenting styles
- Stepfamily expectations and beliefs
- Balancing our needs – costs and rewards
- Parenting styles

Session 3: The couple relationship

A session to help couples strengthen their own relationship and in turn set a strong foundation for the stepfamily.

- The importance of the couple relationship
- Effective communication
- Learning to empathise
- Dealing with stress and anxiety
- Building an integrated stepfamily

Session 4: Developing coping strategies

A session to help the family realise both the importance of external support through family and friends and potential gaps in their support network. Also important to provide effective coping mechanisms for dealing with family stresses.

- Learning to use effective coping strategies
- The importance of social support
- Co-parenting strategies
- What next?

6 MEDIATION

Often the issues faced by couples in stepfamilies are not easily addressed within the immediate family. For example, many issues are unresolved between the biological partners, with these factors impacting the new stepfamily unit. Frequently grandparents can feel excluded from grandchildren when couples separate and relationships become difficult. There are times therefore when it is appropriate to seek mediation when working with stepfamilies. While it is recognised that some therapists may not be able to offer this service to clients it is worthwhile recognising its place within the integrated approach to helping stepfamilies and that some clients may need to be signposted towards it. The mediation process is not defined within this chapter but rather the underlying principles.

The chapter will therefore address the following questions.

- What is mediation?
- What are the benefits of using mediation with stepfamilies and separated couples?
- What skills does the facilitator need to use during the mediation?

I would like to thank Paul Randolph for his assistance in the writing and reviewing of this chapter. Paul is a practising barrister and an Accredited Mediator. He was responsible for co-designing and creating the unique psychotherapeutically informed mediation training (Alternative Dispute Resolution) at Regent's University London, where he now leads and lectures on the course. The training and support Paul has given to me have been invaluable.

Background

Mediation is a process in which individuals use both direct and indirect communication, facilitated by a third party, to resolve ongoing issues. It is used successfully in low- and high-conflict relationships, and serves people across all socioeconomic and ethnic backgrounds. The goal is to move towards a workable agreement, usually in writing if the parties request it. Mediators are trained to identify and work with the key issues related to the ongoing conflict, and to ensure the mediation process supports each individual's understanding. Often they enable options to be generated by the parties for their consideration, and they will try to establish and maintain a balanced and respectful process in order to reach an agreement.

Although there are many applications for mediation, not least in the field of law, mediation related to couple separation and divorce has gained significant attention in recent years. It is now often used as an alternative approach to the adversarial process through the law courts, offering potential lower costs both economically and emotionally (Pruett *et al.*, 2003). Family mediation addresses a number of areas related to the ongoing co-parenting, and often includes timetables for access, decision making related to the children, child support/maintenance, and the division of assets and liabilities.

Mediation can often help better prepare couples for the separation and ongoing relationships with former partners (Severson *et al.*, 2004), allowing for greater collaboration and communication. A 12-year study that compared mediation with litigation (Emery, Sbarra and Grover, 2005) found that mediation led to substantial long-term benefits for parents and children. A review of major family mediation studies suggested that family mediation was successful in resolving custody and access disputes in both process and outcome measures (Kelly, 2004). Pearson and Thoennes (1988) found that individuals who were in mediation were much more satisfied with the process, regardless of whether or not they reached an agreement. There are, however, gender differences. Some research has found that fathers find the mediation approach more satisfactory than those experiencing litigation, while mothers reported more satisfaction with the litigation route, specifically in terms of child outcomes (Emery, Matthews and Wyer, 1991), However women do appear to find the mediation process useful in better understanding their spouse's point of view (Kelly and Gigy, 1989). In terms of the children, couples have reported that mediation has helped them focus on the needs of the children (Pearson and Thoennes, 1988), as well as increase their understanding of their children's psychological needs and reactions (Kelly and Gigy, 1989). Mediation also appears to provide a welcome opportunity for the couple to air grievances and be better able to identify underlying issues (Pearson and Thoennes, 1988), stand up for themselves (Kelly and Gigy, 1989) and perceive a fairness related to the process and the overall outcomes.

Perhaps one of the most important findings related to family mediation is that non-residential parents who had used the mediation route maintained more contact and involvement with their children in comparison with those who used litigation for child custody issues. (Emery *et al.*, 2001). Significant differences were found in terms of frequency of access, telephone contact, influence on the residential parent's decision making, and overall relationship between the non-residential parent and their children in a wide range of activities.

Despite the evidence in support of mediation, however, many couples still choose the legal route when divorcing or separating, often turning to the legal profession and the courts to ultimately enforce decisions related to care of and access to their children. This can lead to ongoing conflict in their co-parenting activities, with parents suffering ongoing animosity and anger towards their ex partners. One of the most powerful forces that drives parties to litigation is the desire to be heard. However, it is generally accepted by those who have been through this process that this objective is rarely achieved (Strasser and Randolph, 2004). In contrast, mediation does offer the opportunity to achieve this goal effectively and consistently.

Unlike the legal system, mediation and therapy have a number of similarities. Mediation encourages communication between the parties; the mediator also encourages collaboration and reflective listening, reframing issues and encouraging the parties to work towards a mutually acceptable outcome. Mediation also emphasises problem solving rather than winning. Collaboration is encouraged, and the mediator seeks to promote a commitment and desire in the parties to identify solutions that are mutually beneficial rather than one family member 'winning'. However, there are also clear differences. Mediation by its very nature involves two parties – rather than one client – and tends to be more acutely goal directed. With therapy, the past is sometimes used to understand the problem, however with mediation it can be used to dispel assumptions and misconceptions, and to discover examples of solutions that can be drawn on in the present.

The object of mediation is to help find a satisfactory solution to a specific area of conflict that is acceptable to all parties, which then allows them to be able to work together more amicably. The solution may involve a paradigm shift in attitude for both parties with an outcome that is 'good enough' for both to accept.

Underlying motivations

One of the most important aspects to the mediation process is for the mediator to explore and understand the underlying reasons for the conflict. With couples trying to navigate the shared care of their children, there are often underlying motivations such as jealousy, anger and hurt that are driving the conflict. Frequently individuals don't acknowledge the underlying reasons for the conflict, having justified their position on other grounds. Often one parent wishes to punish the other for leaving; they may feel jealous that the other parent has 'moved on' and is in another relationship, or may want to assert their authority in the care of the children. Conflicts often flare up with access in general, as well as related to more specific occasions such as holidays, family celebrations and school-related activities such as parents evenings, school plays or even simply picking up the children from school.

One of the considerations during this part of the process is to understand both parties' core beliefs and values, often referred to as their 'worldview'. Individuals make choices based on their value system, which inherently limits their choices. However, they are able to choose and modify this system. While conflict cannot always be eliminated, our attitude or approach to it can be changed.

The concept of 'worldview' is therefore important to the mediation process. In order to facilitate a change in attitude it may be necessary for the mediator to encourage the individual to challenge his or her own worldview. This in turn may help the individual in recognising their underlying motives and drivers, and so facilitate a change in perspective.

Mediator skills

The following sections list some of the key skills that mediators should employ when conducting time-limited mediation.

Table 6.1 Non-verbal cues

Eye contact	Should be natural and engaged
Nodding	Demonstrates that the mediator is still listening, but does not break the flow of speech
Posture	The mediator should, if appropriate, try to lean forwards to demonstrate their engagement; leaning back with arms folded can in many circumstances achieve the opposite!
Interrupting	This is to be avoided if at all possible as it breaks the concentration of the speaker and can then change the direction of conversation; the mediator should allow the party to talk uninterrupted and ask for clarification only when they stop
Silence	This can be the most difficult to achieve but is a powerful tool; leaving space for the party to continue talking or even to think about what they have said can often provide important breakthroughs; mediators are therefore encouraged not to feel the need to fill silence

Active listening

For any successful mediation it can be vital that the mediator convinces each party that they are truly being heard and that the mediator is giving them their full attention. Taking notes, for example, might help the mediator remember the points being made, but this breaks the non-verbal cues so important to showing the client they are being listened to. A list of non-verbal cues is provided in Table 6.1.

Open questions

In order to maximise the responses of the party expressing their views, all questions should be phrased openly, meaning that they can't be answered with a 'no' or 'yes' response. Closed questions, eliciting one-word answers, serve to restrict the flow of information and can lead the party into answering in a socially desirable way.

Reflecting back and paraphrasing

These techniques allow the mediator to feed back what the party has just told them, illustrating that they have been listening attentively and also checking that they have understood them correctly. The mediator's use of words may often be critical here, as they will normally need to maintain the meaning and feeling communicated by the client. For example, if the client has just told the mediator that they were devastated when their partner left them, they may not appreciate being told that they were sad to be on their own. The level of meaning should ideally be matched between client and mediator, although occasionally, by getting it wrong, the mediator can precipitate a clarification from the party, which can in itself be informative.

Summarising

Again, this is a very important part of the mediation and involves giving a summary of the main aspects of the conversation. It can take place at any time during the process, and can be a way of reviewing or even checking that the mediator has understood both the facts and the emotions correctly, particularly when the issues are complex and confusing. When used at the end of a private meeting, a summary can provide a useful indicator for the mediator as to the issues or messages that might helpfully be taken across to the other party.

Empathy

Empathy is a fundamental skill within mediation, establishing rapport and trust between mediator and party. Empathy is an acknowledgement and understanding of another person's position. The mediator therefore needs, as far as possible, to truly stand in the party's shoes, while maintaining independence and neutrality. It is important to separate this from sympathy, which is merely sharing the emotions of others and is not appropriate for mediators. This would remove objectivity and neutrality.

Acceptance and bracketing

This technique is centred around accepting the client's position and being non-judgmental of their stance. The mediator has to accept the party's position and suspend their own opinions. In doing so, the mediator allows the party to feel truly heard.

Identifying themes

More experienced mediators can often find recurring themes hidden within conversations. Parties sometimes repeat the same messages, often unwittingly, revealing issues that are important to them. It may be a simple word or the same issue that keeps resurfacing, either of which might signify potentially greater significance to the party that could be worthy of further exploration.

Challenging/confronting

At some stage within the private meeting, the mediator may need to begin to challenge the party to confront the issues. Some examples follow.

- It may be that they can feed back contradictions or discrepancies in their actions or words, e.g. *You say that your ex partner is a good father and yet you are reluctant to let him spend time alone with his son.*
- The mediator might question the validity of a party's stance, e.g. *So do you think it's the right approach to stop your daughter seeing her father?*
- The mediator might suggest a shift in approach, e.g. *How would you feel about possibly letting your ex see your daughter over Christmas?*
- The mediator might test a number of scenarios using the 'what if' test, e.g. *What if you did let your ex partner see your daughter this weekend? What do you think might happen? Or, alternatively, what might happen if you refuse to let your ex partner see your daughter?*

All of these methods of challenging and reality testing are appropriate, but may work better in different scenarios. However, all must be used cautiously, tentatively and with empathy. They are most effective when used once the mediator has established a good rapport with the party and there is an element of trust. If the techniques are employed too early they may serve only to destroy any semblance of trust and rapport, and take the mediator back to the beginning of the process.

> **Case study: Mediation to agree contact between father and daughter (Part 1 – understanding motivations)**
>
> **David and Anne** came to see me recently and were at a loss to know how to deal with an issue related to David's daughter, **Sophie**, and his ex wife **Ellie**. David and Ellie had split up two years earlier when Sophie was 7. Sophie lived predominantly with Ellie but visited her

dad and his partner every other weekend and on Wednesdays after school. David had recently changed jobs, which made it impossible for him to pick up Sophie from school on a Wednesday, however Anne was more than happy to help out and look after Sophie until her dad came home later in the evening. Anne had done this several times and there had been no problems. Sophie seemed happy to leave with her and they both enjoyed spending some time together. However, Ellie had found out and had now 'banned' Anne from picking up her daughter. She claimed that Sophie was uncomfortable spending time with Anne and would rather go home to her mum's if her dad couldn't pick her up. David was angry and frustrated. He felt there was no issue and was adamant that Anne would continue to pick her up. Anne felt awkward and, while she wanted to support her partner, didn't want to make things worse in her relationship with Sophie. David wanted to seek legal help but Anne had suggested they try mediation. He had agreed to try this approach and had managed to persuade Ellie to attend a meeting.

At this point both parties had entrenched positions. Ellie was adamant that Anne can't pick up her daughter from school, while David was equally adamant that she could. Anne felt caught in the middle and we can only presume that Sophie felt this conflict in some way.

The approach adopted by the mediator in this case was to talk to David and Ellie individually, to explore their feelings and views in order to reveal the underlying motivations. Was Sophie really unhappy about Anne picking her up? Or was Ellie perhaps jealous of Anne and worried about 'sharing' her role in some way? Perhaps she felt David should have sole responsibility for Sophie? Did she agree with the arrangements for access to Sophie? Perhaps she wanted Sophie with her during the school week and had never been happy with this arrangement?

Case study: Mediation to agree contact between father and daughter (Part 2 – the mediation process)

David and Ellie arrived to see me for the planned mediation. I introduced myself and explained the process. We had scheduled 90 minutes to discuss the topic of midweek access for David with Sophie. The aim was to find a mutually agreeable solution, without the need to seek legal advice.

I explained to them both how the process would work, with initial separate meetings for them each to discuss their position and views. The discussion within these meetings would be confidential and not shared by me with the other party without their express permission.

I then asked each of them in turn to explain the issue, as they perceived it, and their stance. After that, I asked whether they wished to say anything further to each other at that stage by way of 'reply', or whether they preferred not to debate this, but rather just to listen to the other person. I then explained why I would see Ellie first, and asked Ellie to remain in the room while I escorted David to another room. When I returned to Ellie, I reassured her that everything we talked about was confidential and asked her to tell me more about the problem. She explained that she just didn't think it was 'right' for Anne to be involved with the school and picking up Sophie. Sophie was still very young and still getting used to mummy and daddy not being together. If Anne started picking her up from school then Sophie might be confused about Anne's role. She also felt very strongly that it was up to David to care for Sophie – if he couldn't look after her then she shouldn't be going to visit on Wednesdays. I told Ellie that I thought it must have been very difficult for her to cope when she split up with David, managing on her own with Sophie for the majority of the time. I asked her if she missed Sophie when she was at David's. She began telling me how lonely she had been since the split, she missed Sophie and it really hurt her to think her daughter was with 'another woman' when she could have been with her. I asked her what she thought of Anne and whether she believed she was ultimately a good carer of Sophie. Ellie admitted that she did like Anne but could only think of her as David's partner – not anything to do with Sophie. We explored some of these areas further, in particular Ellie's view on family and roles. It transpired that Ellie was struggling to accept the changes. She wanted David to maintain a good relationship with Sophie, but did not see why she had to give up time for Anne to spend time with her daughter. I tried to encourage Ellie to consider the consequences of allowing the visits to go ahead. How would she feel if Anne continued to pick up Sophie? How would Sophie react? Would there be any impact on her relationship with David, and how might that be perceived by Sophie? During this time Ellie said that she really wanted David to continue to play a big role in Sophie's life. She knew he was a good dad and Sophie missed him when he wasn't there. I felt this was a really positive message and would be helpful for David to hear, so I asked if she agreed. She did, and allowed me to repeat this to David. I left her to consider the 'what if' scenarios and went to meet with David.

I began the session by asking David to tell me about the issue from his perspective. He explained that the split from Ellie had been difficult but they had both largely agreed that each of them should continue to play a major role in Sophie's life. I took this opportunity to let him know that Ellie had told me what a good dad he was and how much she wanted him to remain involved in bringing up Sophie. He appreciated this and said that he felt the same about Ellie. She was a great mum to Sophie but things had really only changed when he had met Anne and they had begun to argue more, particularly around his time with Sophie. He was very angry that Ellie had made these conditions regarding his access on Wednesdays, frustrated that she felt she had more overall control. He felt he needed to go to court to 'prove' to her that they were equal parents and it was his right to arrange cover for childcare as needed. I empathised with him regarding the split, agreeing that this must have been very painful, especially now that he sees Sophie only part-time. He told me how sad he feels and how much he looks forward to seeing her, especially on a Wednesday when he sometimes hasn't seen her for a week. When he moved jobs recently it was frustrating that he couldn't leave on time to pick her up from school, but he always made sure he was back in time for them to eat dinner together and spend time with her before bedtime.

I then asked him to consider what would happen if Anne didn't pick up Sophie on a Wednesday. He explained that he just wouldn't be able to see her, which would mean then seeing her only every other weekend. He felt that this would be difficult for him and for Sophie. While he didn't want to change the agreement he did say that he thought he would be able to leave work early regularly on a Friday – but he didn't see why he should have to change, just because Ellie wanted to. I felt that this could be a solution and asked if I could possibly share these thoughts with Ellie. I also wanted to ask if I could tell Ellie what David had said about her role as a mother. At first he was reluctant about offering the alternative option, but then said I could, but only if I felt the Wednesday access was not going to be possible. I thanked him and moved back to talk to Ellie.

I started the second session by asking if Ellie had had any thoughts while she was alone. She said that she was glad she had agreed to the mediation, as it was the first time since David had met Anne that they had talked without arguing. She felt he had changed and no longer appreciated how hard it was for her bringing up Sophie. I took the opportunity to share with her what David had said about her being such a good mum and then began to explore again her views on the Wednesday access. She said that she felt things were happening too quickly with Anne but didn't want Sophie to miss out on seeing her dad. She said that she didn't really know Anne and it felt awkward hearing her daughter speak about someone she didn't know. I asked if it would help if she met her for a coffee. Ellie said that she thought that would be a good idea and was willing to give it all another try. At this point I asked Ellie whether she thought it would be worth bringing her and David together to discuss a way forward. She thought it would, and so I indicated I would need to check with David whether he was similarly comfortable with a joint session at that stage. David agreed to have a joint session.

During the joint meeting it was agreed that Ellie and Anne would meet before Wednesday and that Anne could continue picking up Sophie. It was also agreed that Ellie and David would meet in another month's time to check that Sophie is OK.

The process was completed within the time allocated, and both David and Ellie felt comfortable with the outcome. Ellie felt that she had been listened to and was able to feel more relaxed about Anne's involvement in Sophie's life. She recognised that Anne wasn't a threat to her in any way and was a positive influence in Sophie's life. David had maintained the contact with Sophie he wanted but had shown Ellie that he respected her and recognised her role as mother and primary caregiver.

Conclusion and key learning points

This chapter has sought to describe a mediation process that can form a key intervention in the support of divorced couples with children, and the related issues felt when these individuals find new partners and form stepfamilies. Many of the issues experienced within the new stepfamily are related to ongoing conflict between the biological parents and, as the case study presented in this chapter illustrates, may be exacerbated by the involvement of new partners.

7 CASE STUDIES

This chapter introduces a number of case studies, chosen to represent the different types of stepfamily (in terms of family complexity and residency) and the integrated approach to therapy. Examples of both stepmother- and stepfather-led families have been included, together with a same-sex couple.

Case study 1: Sarah and Gary (simple part-time, stepmother and biological father)

Sarah and Gary represent one of the most common types of stepfamily seeking support. It is interesting to note, however, that these families are often excluded from national statistics and overall stepfamily figures due to the lack of residency of the children. Part-time stepmothers often have higher anxiety than other stepfamily members, related to their role in the family, their lack of confidence with their stepchildren, and the ongoing interference or influence of the biological mother (Doodson and Davies, 2014). The therapist's goals therefore are often best targeted at providing help for the stepmother in order to reduce overall anxiety, and help identify a clear and appropriate role for her within the family unit. This particular case study illustrates the use of couple therapy combined with mediation involving the biological parents to facilitate agreement in relation to co-parenting.

Stage 1: Initial assessment

Family description

Sarah and Gary have been together for five years and married for the past two. Gary is 40 years old and Sarah 33. Sarah had not been married before and had no prior children. Gary was married previously, to Emily for three years, but was single for a year prior to his relationship with Sarah. Emily and Gary had a child together, Holly, who was now 7 years old. They separated within the first year of Holly's life and their relationship has been acrimonious ever since. Emily had not wanted to have children but had been persuaded by Gary. She had suffered badly from postnatal depression following the birth and had struggled to bond with Holly in the early stages. However, since the split, Emily has taken on primary care for her daughter and Gary sees his daughter regularly.

Sarah and Gary had a baby together just under a year ago and, since then, Sarah has not worked (by choice). Gary is self-employed and work is generally going well. Sarah is now pregnant with her second child. They have told Holly and she is happy. Emily has not remarried and has no long-term partner. She lives alone with Holly.

Timeline

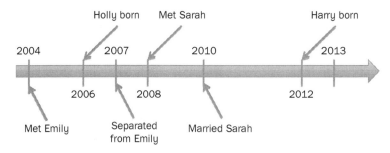

Figure 7.1 Timeline – Gary

Co-parenting arrangements

Gary's separation from Emily had been extremely acrimonious and had necessitated many court visits in order to establish access arrangements for Holly. Emily's mental wellbeing was affected significantly following the birth of her daughter, however on separation from Gary she was adamant that she was going to be the primary carer. Gary had instigated the separation and Emily was reluctant to allow him access to Holly. Consequently, after a lengthy series of court battles, he had secured regular weekly access and holidays. However, Emily frequently prevented the visits, seemingly because Holly was unwilling to go to her father's house. Gary had persevered and, when he first came to see me, the visits were regular but fraught with difficulties.

Emily insisted that Gary was the only one that was allowed to pick up Holly from school. While in general this worked well, occasionally he was delayed with work commitments. Sarah, Gary's wife, was more than happy to pick Holly up from school but felt this was always going to cause arguments with Emily at a later date. There was little scope for a change in arrangements: whenever Gary requested such a change it was generally rejected and caused further conflict. Consequently, the adults were all conforming to the formal court agreement. However, holidays were becoming problematic. While Gary and Sarah tried to arrange these well in advance, Emily always seemed to object and make things extremely difficult for them to plan their time away with Holly. The latest issues had resolved around Emily saying that she could not let Holly leave for longer than five consecutive days as she would miss her mother too much. When they did take Holly away, Emily would phone every day, often several times a day. Holly's behaviour would change during and after these calls, becoming more secretive and difficult.

Sarah and Gary were becoming increasingly frustrated by their inability to make plans both on a weekly basis and for family holidays.

Since the split from Emily, Gary had been paying a generous agreed amount of maintenance to Emily. The amount had been agreed by the court.

Relationships

Gary and Sarah presented as a very strong couple. They were very supportive of each other and perceived the same issues within their family. Sarah was the one who initially approached me, however Gary was very supportive and eager to play an active role in the counselling sessions.

In terms of the biological relationships, Sarah did not have any prior significant relationships and had no prior children. Consequently this was not a major area of enquiry or concern for the ensuing counselling sessions. Gary and Emily however clearly had a very difficult, acrimonious relationship. Emily was very bitter following the spilt from Gary and was making it very difficult for Gary and Sarah to develop their relationship with Holly. The households appeared to be in similar socioeconomic groups and neither appeared to have any significant financial constraints.

The relationship between Gary and his daughter Holly was very close, however Gary displayed a level of guilt at having 'abandoned' his daughter. This affected his ability to discipline her consistently. In return, she was clearly aware that she could manipulate her father more effectively than her stepmother, leading to inequalities in the household.

Sarah had developed a good relationship with Holly and they appeared to enjoy each other's company. Sarah was very eager to ensure they maintained consistent family rules, particularly since the birth of Harry, her son with Gary. While Sarah had a genuine affection for Holly she was frustrated at her behaviour at times and felt that she and Gary were inconsistent in reacting to bad behaviour. In general Sarah enjoyed having Holly in their home, however she had begun to resent the way their time as a family was being dictated by Emily. She was also frustrated at the difficulties they were having in organising holidays and the impact Emily then had on their time together through excessive telephone calls and contact with Holly.

Holly did not have any siblings with her mother, but now had Harry as a half brother. She seemed to enjoy being able to help look after Harry, and did not appear to hold any resentment to him or his place in the household. She regularly helped Gary and Sarah in looking after Harry.

Stage 2: Magic question – prioritise issues

Both Gary and Sarah had two areas they wanted help with. The first was in dealing with Emily's unreasonable behaviour. They both felt that she was constantly dictating what they could and couldn't do – from who could pick Holly up from school to when they could take her on holiday.

The second issue was related to Holly. They were both struggling with her behaviour at times but were finding it difficult to discipline her effectively. On a recent holiday, she kicked a family friend when she was angry. Her temper appears to be an issue and she doesn't seem to be able to control herself appropriately. They gave another example where she had drawn on the wall in her bedroom. When they told her off she became very upset but did not seem to understand why she was being told off. Gary then found it difficult to deal with her crying and effectively 'let her off' as far as Sarah was concerned. They both felt they wanted to be consistent in their parenting of Holly.

Stage 3: Interventions

I spent some of the first session reassuring Sarah and Gary that their experiences were completely normal and common, particularly in relation to the influence of the ex partner, and their differences in parenting styles and approaches. The couple had only been together a relatively short time and within this time had extended their family with the birth of their son. I explained that in any family, step or biological, a new baby is also bound to bring changes and potential issues with existing children. I encouraged them to focus on the more immediate problem of Holly's anger and behaviour, which was within their control. We would discuss Gary's relationship with Emily at a later date.

Holly's behaviour had been quite problematic for the couple in recent months. Sarah explained that the last episode, where she had drawn on the wall in her bedroom, had been the final straw. She had gone into Holly's room to find she had drawn in coloured pen on the wall. She immediately told Holly off and Holly reacted by crying. She didn't offer any explanation about why she had done it and didn't apologise to Sarah. When Gary came back from work, Sarah explained what had happened and he had gone to see Holly in her room. Sarah felt that he had then not supported her but had merely comforted Holly. Gary explained that he felt he could not cope when Holly cried; he just wanted to make her feel better. While she spent a reasonable amount of time at her father and Sarah's house, he felt guilty that his son was with them all the time while Holly only visited. In a separate incident Holly had become angry at a recent family get-together and ended up hitting one of the adults when she didn't get her own way. Both Gary and Sarah had been shocked and immediately reprimanded her, however Sarah felt it was she who had had to assume the leading role and Gary had quickly turned from being angry to being supportive of Holly when she subsequently cried.

We discussed the importance of setting clear boundaries with Holly and her receiving consistent discipline – from both of them. While they both agreed with this principle, Gary explained that in practice he found it very difficult to be the disciplinarian. In his past relationship it had been Emily who had taken on this role, and the same pattern was emerging in his relationship with Sarah. I took this as an opportunity to discuss their roles within the stepfamily. I felt that Sarah had adopted a strong parenting role with Holly and she confirmed that she was happy to take a more proactive and involved role. Gary was equally happy and supportive for Sarah to assume this role with Holly. However, I pointed out to Gary that, in order for this to work, Sarah needed his full support otherwise any rules or discipline she tried to assume with Holly would be undermined.

I reassured them that the main point was that they were both in agreement; it was a matter of modifying their own behaviour if things were to improve. I suggested that they spend some time discussing and setting house rules and what each felt would be appropriate punishment, to ensure they could be consistent in dealing with future problems with Holly. They also needed to send out a clear message to Holly on their expectations of her.

Over several sessions the couple were able to make significant improvements in jointly parenting Holly, through clearer rules and consequences. Gary had avoided comforting Holly after she had misbehaved but had reinforced the messages given by Sarah. As such, both felt that Holly's behaviour had become more manageable, resulting in a calmer household.

We then moved on in later sessions to discuss the difficulties the couple were having with Emily. Sarah felt that she had very little control over their own lives, being dictated to on what they could and couldn't do with Holly. Holidays were a particular pressure point, where in recent months Emily had told Gary that they couldn't take Holly on a holiday lasting longer than five days as it would be too distressing for her and she would not be able to cope without seeing her mother for longer. Both Sarah and Gary were very frustrated and felt powerless. Holidays were important family times for them and they both wanted Holly to be part of them. These unrealistic demands were making holidays difficult to plan and understandably causing friction between Sarah and Gary. Unless the couple learned to accept the restrictions imposed on them for holidays, the only resolution to this issue needed to involve Gary's ex wife. We agreed that Gary would approach Emily to suggest a mediation session to discuss her worries over longer holidays. She agreed and I set up a mediation session between the three of us. I spoke to Gary's ex wife prior to the session to reassure her of my impartiality and to explain the process to her.

In addition to this, I spent some time during one session in helping Sarah and Gary focus on what they could achieve within their family unit. Due to the ongoing animosity between Gary and his ex wife, they had been spending a great deal of time and effort in discussing Gary's ex rather than simply enjoying their time together as a family. They both learned to accept that there were aspects of Holly's life that they were unable to control and to focus more on what they could control.

Stage 4: Homework

In between the sessions, I encouraged the couple to keep a diary of events and feelings, particularly focusing on things that had caused arguments or problems in the family. These could then be discussed at future sessions, and we were able to discuss alternative approaches and possible outcomes.

Sarah was also eager for reassurance in her role and care of Holly. Gary was the more placid of the two and as such tended to defer to Sarah in the care of Holly. Sarah therefore needed a boost in her confidence and self-esteem to support her in her role of stepmother. I suggested a couple of self-help books that would help to normalise her experiences.

Current situation

Sarah and Gary came to see me for eight sessions, spread over a period of 18 months. They have since had another child together and are coping well. They have maintained the access arrangements with Holly and her behaviour is improving. Gary and Sarah have maintained a 'united front' in terms of discipline and have been rewarded with more consistent behaviour from Holly. They have also spent several happy family holidays together – all longer than five days! The relationship between Gary and Emily remains strained but workable.

Case study 2: Karen and Tom (simple full-time, biological mother and stepfather)

Karen and Tom represent the most common type of stepfather family, with children residing in the home for the majority of the time. While they are the most commonly reported stepfamily type, they are less likely than other stepfamily types to seek external support. Common issues faced by this family type are frequently related to clarifying the stepfather role in the family, particularly with respect to discipline and their involvement with the stepchildren, and normalising their experiences. The therapist's goals therefore are often best targeted at helping the couple set clear foundations for the new family unit, and negotiating roles and responsibilities for the adults.

Stage 1: Initial assessment

Family description

Karen and Tom have been together for the past two years, however they have known each other for 12 years, having first met at university. Karen was previously married to John, whom she also met at university, and they had two children together: Alex aged 6 and Maddie aged 8. Tom and John were good friends and Tom is also godfather to Alex.

When I met the couple they had already spent a significant amount of time in family therapy, however they felt that things had not really improved, and they felt 'stuck' and unable to move on in their relationship.

Tom feels disloyal to John. While he and Karen did not become a couple until the relationship between Karen and John had finished, he feels he 'got in the way of the marriage and the children'. The children have developed a good relationship with Tom but he is unable to enjoy them as he is consumed with guilt.

Tom has not told colleagues about his relationship with Karen. He does not seem to have accepted the situation and does not relate to being a stepfamily. He feels it is all morally wrong and is unable to move on.

Timeline

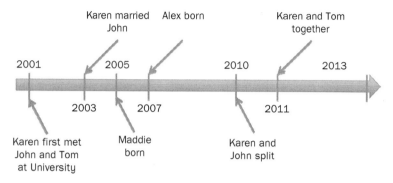

Figure 7.2 Timeline – Karen and Tom

Co-parenting arrangements

Karen and John have an amicable arrangement with the children. While the children spend the majority of time with their mother, they see John regularly at weekends and holidays. John and Karen are able to talk rationally about the children and there does not seem to be any ongoing animosity or anger between them. As such the children seem relatively settled and happy with both parents. The arrangements are all fairly informal and not dictated by any formal court agreements.

Relationships

Karen and Tom appear to have a very close and balanced relationship. While their current romantic relationship is relatively new, they have a strong history between them and know each other very well. This means that they have very mature communication skills, however while they can discuss the issues they are at a loss as to how to address them.

Karen and John's relationship appears to have run its natural course and as such they both appear to be content following their separation. John appears to hold no malice towards Tom, however Tom is finding it difficult to accept a role within the stepfamily.

Karen has a very close bond with both children. There don't appear to be any particular issues with their behaviour. Tom has a good relationship with both children, however he seems to struggle with taking on any role other than godparent with them.

Stage 2: Magic question

The only real issue that Tom and Karen were struggling with was how to find a way for Tom to fully accept his role in the stepfamily. His feelings of guilt and morality continue to plague him and prevent him from taking a more integrated role in the new stepfamily.

Stage 3: Intervention

My initial focus with Karen and Tom was in trying to get them to replace their expectations with more realistic goals. While the couple had known each other for a long time, their romantic relationship was still relatively new. This shift in relationship was clearly difficult for Tom to cope with so I encouraged them both to stop putting pressure on themselves to create this new 'instant family', which Karen was eager to do. Tom didn't want to feel as though he was replacing John in any way – as a friend he continued to feel guilty that he was spending more time with the children than their father was. I helped them understand that they were still in the early stages of their relationship and time would help them all find their role within the new unit.

Tom clearly had a very negative view of stepfamilies and found it extremely difficult to accept that he was effectively now part of one. We used one session to talk about stepfamilies and why Tom felt so negatively about them. To him, the term signified some sort of failure in a previous family. He had no experience of family breakdowns in his own upbringing and felt embarrassed about being associated with one. We talked about the increase in stepfamilies in society and what factors drive that – for example, the choices couples have and the financial freedom that allows couples to live apart when relationships break down. I explained that all stepfamilies are different but that the most important aspect for children is to maintain good relationships with both parents.

We also then spent some time exploring roles. My purpose was to understand what role Tom wanted within the family and, similarly, what Karen's views were. It became clear that the couple had very different expectations in this area – Karen felt that Tom should be taking on a parenting role, whereas Tom felt far more comfortable as a 'family friend'. He did not want to get involved in disciplining the children, for example, as he felt this was not his job. In fact, any aspects of the role that seemed to overlap with John's made him feel incredibly uncomfortable.

We discussed what aspects of his role with the children he was comfortable with being involved in. Tom explained that he enjoyed spending time with them, playing and helping them, but simply felt uncomfortable when this role overlapped with a more traditional parenting role.

I suggested that the couple spend more time together as a family, building memories and increasing Tom's confidence. I urged them to stop putting undue pressure on Tom in the short term but to concentrate on recognising the many positives in their relationship: Tom had a close relationship with the children, having known them all their lives, John appeared to have accepted their relationship, and contact was agreed and stable.

Stage 4: Homework

I also felt that Tom might benefit from talking to John. The two had been good friends, and one of the barriers in Tom's relationship with Karen and the children was the fact that he might be hurting John and replacing him in some way. We discussed the possibility of the two men meeting, and Tom letting John know how he felt and reassuring him that he didn't want to take his place in any way but simply wanted to help care for the children. Tom took some time to think about this but after a couple of sessions felt that this might be helpful. The meeting went ahead and, while Tom was apprehensive and nervous, he found it very beneficial.

Current situation

I saw Karen and Tom four times over a period of six months. Tom was becoming more comfortable in his role supporting Karen. He had maintained contact with John and saw him regularly for a drink. He was still reluctant to discipline the children but the couple had instilled a number of house rules that Tom was happy to maintain with Karen.

Case study 3: Caroline and Simon (complex part-time, both adults taking on biological and stepparent roles)

Caroline and Simon represent a complex stepfamily, where both adults bring children with them from previous relationships. Often the children also visit their other biological parents, requiring the adults to maintain excellent communication with their partners to remove any confusion and ambiguity in arrangements and expectations. One of the key challenges for this type of family is the integration of their new family and the acceptance of their partner's children. Given that both adults have parenting experience they often have the confidence and ability to parent within the stepfamily and there are fewer changes to their lifestyle in order to adapt to the new family unit. The therapist's goals therefore are often best targeted at helping both adults build better relationships with their stepchildren.

Stage 1: Initial assessment

Family description

Simon and Caroline have been together as a couple for five years. Simon has two children from his previous marriage, Alice aged 18 and Oliver aged 15. Caroline has a son, Ben, aged 7 from her previous marriage. The couple had an affair while both were with their previous partners and left their marriages to be together.

Both Simon and Caroline's family (parents and siblings) live abroad so are not able to support them practically.

Caroline and Simon live together with Caroline's son, who visits his father regularly. Simon's children live with their mother, and visit their father and Caroline irregularly.

Timeline

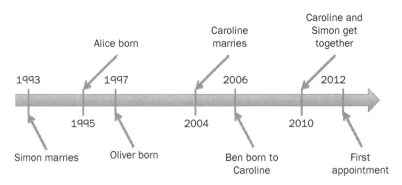

Figure 7.3   Timeline – Caroline and Simon

Co-parenting arrangements

Caroline and her ex have maintained a good relationship and have a flexible shared care arrangement over Ben.

Simon however has a very difficult relationship with his ex wife, Evie. She is still bitter and angry over the split, and holds both Simon and Caroline responsible. Consequently communication between Simon and Evie is extremely difficult. The divorce and access was very acrimonious and while the court order allows Simon to have access to the children at weekends, this is happening only rarely as the children are reluctant to visit.

Relationships

Simon and Caroline have a very loving yet volatile relationship. They are clearly very much in love but are also prone to explosive arguments. Communication is difficult as, when there is disagreement, neither is willing to compromise.

Caroline has a very close relationship with her son, Ben, and is protective of him. He appears to be a well-behaved little boy and has coped well following his parents' split.

Simon was close to both of his children prior to the separation from his ex wife, however since he has been living with Caroline, both the relationships are difficult. His daughter will speak to him over the phone but refuses to come to his new home with Caroline. She will meet him, but strictly on her terms. Oliver will come and visit Simon and stay for weekends, however he refuses to interact with Caroline. He is polite, however, and will always answer her when she talks to him.

Caroline's relationship with Simon's children is therefore very difficult. She has barely met Alice and when Oliver visits she finds it very hard to communicate with him. Simon, though, has a good relationship with Ben and there appear to be no issues here.

Oliver does not really interact with Ben – with an eight-year age gap there is very little in common between the boys. However Caroline is disappointed that Oliver doesn't try harder as Ben has come to enjoy his visits and really looks forward to seeing him. She feels sorry for Ben when he is ignored.

Stage 2: Magic question

Both Simon and Caroline wanted help in improving Caroline's relationship with Oliver. While Oliver visited his father and Caroline's house fairly regularly, the visits were awkward and difficult due to the lack of communication between Oliver and Caroline. The visits also sparked arguments between Caroline and Simon as they disagreed on how to deal with Oliver's behaviour.

Simon also wanted to improve his relationship with his daughter, whom he was barely seeing, however we agreed to make this a secondary priority and work together on improving the relationship between Oliver and Caroline first.

Stage 3: Intervention

Simon and Caroline had been together for about two years when they first came to see me. They were both frustrated and disappointed about the poor relationship between Caroline and Oliver. Given the fact that Simon's daughter was currently not visiting at all, this meant that Simon was even more protective of his relationship with Oliver. Caroline felt that he 'let Oliver get away with murder' because of this and the ongoing guilt he felt following leaving his ex wife. Caroline felt that Oliver was spoilt and rude, and she was keen to impose clear house rules. She worried that he was becoming a bad influence on her young son with his behaviour while in their home.

The first sessions were spent discussing their expectations as a new stepfamily. Their relationship had been born out of a sudden loss in their previous relationships and, while they had made this choice willingly, their children would take longer to understand and accept the changes. In particular Oliver and Alice were older and more aware of what had happened. It is reasonable to assume that they had seen their mother upset and angry, and this would be difficult for them to deal with, perhaps understandably blaming their father for the hurt. Ben, on the other hand, was much younger and could have been shielded from most of the difficulties. Teenagers are much more likely to take longer to accept a stepparent, particularly if they feel they are in some way responsible for the separation of their parents. I suggested that they give the older children more time and space to deal with the changes and hope that, in time, Alice would be able to come and spend time with her father and Caroline.

In terms of Oliver, we discussed the fact that he may well be dealing with loyalty conflicts, which were affecting his relationship with Caroline. The fact that he had maintained contact was clearly a positive, and not necessarily an easy decision for him given his sister's lack of contact. He may perceive that he is being disloyal to his mother by simply visiting his father and I suggested that his lack of communication with Caroline is related to his feelings of guilt/divided loyalty towards his mother and therefore a desire not to become too close to her.

Given that Oliver's presence in the house was causing so many of the arguments and difficulties in the family I felt it was important that there was agreement over the key issues. We could then work out a plan to minimise the issues and set clear expectations and boundaries. Caroline was understandably hurt when Oliver wouldn't interact easily with her, however she did understand that this behaviour was probably rooted in feelings of guilt towards his mother and loyalty conflicts. She was eager to change the pattern that had developed with his visits. Apparently he was spending the vast majority of his time in his bedroom, playing computer games. When he did come downstairs it was generally just to eat and occasionally watch TV with Simon. When he was with them Caroline felt left out and generally spent the time playing with Ben.

I suggested that the couple begin to plan activities to do at weekends that could involve both Oliver and Ben – for example, walks in the park, visits to the cinema or bowling. The aim should be to plan one activity every weekend that they all took part in. Ideally, Oliver should be involved in the decision and given choices to encourage him to take part.

I also felt the couple needed to find some compromise in terms of acceptable behaviour and to define some basic house rules. For example, Caroline felt that Oliver spent too long playing computer games in his room. However, Simon was reluctant to ask him to change in case he chose not to visit at all. He felt he had already 'lost' his daughter and didn't want to do anything that might make Oliver unwilling to visit. I suggested that the couple spend some time between our meetings putting together a brief list of areas of contention, where they felt they would benefit from guidance. We could then discuss these at subsequent sessions.

Over time we managed to put together a list of basic house rules that both adults felt were reasonable to expect Oliver to live by when he visited. Both agreed that they would enforce these and support each other as necessary. I also encouraged them to spend less time divided along biological lines – Caroline and Ben, and Simon and Oliver – as this was not helping with the integration of the family. The age and gender of Oliver made it more natural for him to seek out the company of his father, which made it all the harder for Caroline to develop her relationship with Oliver. However, over time, Oliver seemed to become less hostile towards Caroline. The four of them started spending more time at weekends together and the family dynamics improved such that after several months Alice began visiting their home.

Stage 4: Homework

Caroline and Simon were tasked with finding activities to do as a family when Oliver came to visit. They had got into a pattern where Caroline would avoid being in the house when Oliver came to visit, so I felt it was important that they all spend time together if their relationships were to improve over time.

Current situation

I saw Simon and Caroline over a two-year period with 15 appointments. They still have a volatile relationship but are happy together and have a good relationship with all the children. Caroline still becomes frustrated at times at the amount of time Simon spends with Oliver in isolation, however this is 'work in progress'. The couple have moved into a larger family home and are considering extending their family.

Case study 4: Jane and Emma (simple part-time, stepmother and biological mother, same-sex couple)

Jane and Emma are an example of a simple same-sex stepfamily. It is estimated that about 1 per cent of all couples living together are same sex (Ambert, 2005). According to some researchers, homosexual parents may face a 'triple stigmatisation': stigmatised for being gay/lesbian, for being a stepfamily and for combining parenthood with homosexuality (Berger, 1998; Lynch, 2005). In addition, they typically experience less support from family than do their heterosexual counterparts (Crosbie-Burnett and Helmbrecht, 1993; Kurdek, 2004). However, levels of happiness and stability in gay and lesbian couples are very similar to those in heterosexual couples (Gottman et al., 2003). Lesbian couples in stepfamilies have also been shown to display higher levels of flexibility, lower levels of reactivity and higher levels of family cohesion than their heterosexual counterparts (Lynch, 2005).

The challenges faced by gay and lesbian stepfamilies are essentially the same as those experienced by heterosexual couples, however they face additional difficulties, too. The children of lesbian and gay step couples experience similar losses and loyalty binds as their counterparts in heterosexual stepfamilies but in addition may have to deal with issues such as stigmatisation, bullying and teasing. However, children in same-sex stepfamilies often fare better on a number of measures and outcomes, including social skills, academic competence, social problems, rule breaking and externalising problem behaviour (Gartrell and Bos, 2010). There is also evidence that gay and lesbian parents' perceptions of stepfamily relationships are more closely aligned with their children's than those in heterosexual stepfamilies (Papernow, 2013).

Turning to parenting challenges, there is evidence that lesbian step couples are more easily able to place children's needs ahead of those of adults, with stepparents in these families more willing early on in the relationship to step back from assuming disciplinary roles (Lynch, 2000). Dealing with homophobia adds a further burden for these families as they try to protect their children from potential stigma and bullying. Conversely, constantly debating how much to share and discuss with those outside the family actually helps build more cohesion within the family, and has been shown to strengthen family closeness and bonding (Lynch, 2005).

Jane and Emma had been in a relationship for two years. They were not only dealing with the 'triple stigma' identified above but had an additional complexity of cultural conflict. Jane, a white British woman, had been married to a man of Asian background. The couple also had very different religious beliefs. Consequently, a lesbian couple was now raising their mixed-race child, which was against the father's religious background. The therapist's goals in this complex case were to deal with the different layers presenting themselves, dealing with the stepfamily-related issues primarily, and then offering further support to address underlying sexuality and cultural issues as needed.

Stage 1: Initial assessment

Family description

Jane and Emma have been together as a couple for less than two years. Jane has one child, Max, aged 2, from a previous marriage. Emma has no children. Both Jane and Emma have had very little support from their wider families, who struggled with their sexuality and choice of partner.

Max lives predominantly with Jane and Emma but visits his biological father on a weekly basis.

Timeline

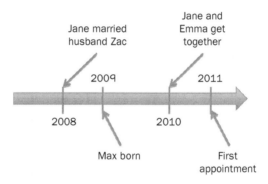

Figure 7.4 Timeline – Jane and Emma

Co-parenting arrangements

Jane and her ex, Zac, continue to have a very conflictual relationship. While Max lives predominantly with Jane, he visits Zac on a weekly basis. Zac disapproves of Jane's relationship with Emma and refuses to acknowledge their status as a couple. Emma has no recent ex and no children.

Relationships

Jane and Emma appear to have a very close relationship, despite its newness, and Emma is very supportive of Jane and Max. Emma enjoys spending time with Max and is happy to take on a parental responsibility when he is living with them. Both Emma and Jane have established clear household rules and roles, and these appear to be working well.

Max enjoys spending time with both his mum and Emma, and appears very settled. His relationship with his father is also close, however Zac appears to have a much less disciplined approach.

Stage 2: Magic question

Emma initially approached me for advice on being a stepmum. She felt that things were going well but recognised that stepfamilies have unique challenges. She was also aware that as a lesbian couple they had additional issues and potential prejudice to deal with, and as such wanted to be as prepared as possible. She asked if it would be possible to attend a series of workshops in a group setting, however they wanted to attend separately as they did not want to attract unnecessary attention or prejudice from other couples. I felt this would provide a good level of support for them both. They did not have any particular issues that they were struggling with. The main issue was related to Jane's ex and their different views on bringing up their son, coupled with different religious backgrounds.

Stage 3: Intervention

Emma and Jane joined a series of weekly workshops, allowing them to learn about common stepfamily pressures, together with effective coping mechanisms. They also met other couples, which reaffirmed that they were coping well and developing a close, integrated family unit. During the first two sessions they sat apart and did not tell the other participants that they were a couple, however as they got to know everyone and felt more comfortable, they let everyone know their situation and why they had felt it necessary to hide their relationship. The rest of the participants were very supportive and this helped give Jane and Emma the strength to continue.

I continued to see Emma and Jane occasionally, however their issues were essentially related to the ongoing animosity between Jane and Zac.

Stage 4: Homework

Homework was provided between each of the workshop sessions. This included making time for their own relationship and going on a date, discussing the roles and responsibilities they wanted to establish in their family unit, and understanding the range of coping mechanisms they were familiar with and felt comfortable with. Examples of some of the exercises used are provided at the end of Chapter 5.

Current situation

Emma and Jane are coping well with the challenges of being a stepfamily. Max is well adjusted and still spends time with his father in addition to the time with Jane and Emma. Last year Emma and Jane decided to get married and I was delighted to be invited to the ceremony! They continue to experience difficulties with Jane's ex but deal with the issues together and ensure that Max is distanced from any conflict.

Case study 5: Lucy and John (simple part-time, stepmother and biological father)

Lucy and John are a further example of the simple stepmother type, however this couple had been together a relatively short amount of time when I met them. I have included this case study as it presents a good example of how situations and issues can change over time, requiring different approaches and interventions. I worked with Lucy and John initially and helped them develop a strong foundation for their new family unit. However, two years later, the couple contacted me again with behavioural issues involving one of John's children.

Stage 1: Initial assessment

Family description

Lucy and John have been together as a couple for two years. John has three children from his previous marriage, Josh aged 13, Cara aged 10 and Lily aged 8. Lucy has no biological children. Lucy's family all live abroad and she has lived in the UK for only three years, so has limited support from family and friends.

Lucy and John have recently moved in together and have John's three children come to stay with them regularly, currently six days out of every 14.

Timeline

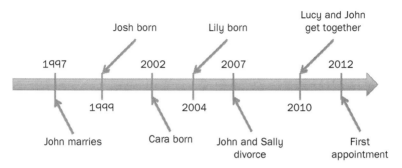

Figure 7.5 Timeline – Lucy and John

Co-parenting arrangements

John and his ex, Sally, have maintained a reasonable relationship and have a flexible shared care arrangement over the children. There appears to be no ongoing conflict, and Sally appears fairly relaxed and happy with Lucy's new role in the family. Lucy has no recent relationships, other than with John, and no prior children.

Relationships

John and Lucy appear to have a very close and loving relationship. John appears very supportive of Lucy and happy to be led by her needs in the sessions. John has a good relationship with all his children and has maintained regular, extensive contact with them since separating from their mother. In the relatively short time she has known the children, Lucy has clearly developed a very good relationship with all three of them. She speaks very lovingly about all the children and does not present any issues in her relationship with them. She does seem sad, however, when she talks about her own family (parents and siblings), who live abroad. She only moved to the UK three years ago with work, and at time feels isolated and lonely.

Stage 2: Magic question

Lucy wanted to feel less resentful of her role. She is embarrassed that she feels this way and doesn't quite understand why. She is also frustrated at John's lack of discipline with the children, which inevitably means she is left with the task. She also feels somewhat overwhelmed by the role and doesn't really understand the boundaries. John, on the other hand, is really attending the sessions only to help Lucy. He doesn't think there are any issues but thinks it is simply a case of giving Lucy more confidence. He believes that this will come over time but nevertheless is happy to come to the sessions if it helps her.

Stage 3: Intervention

The first session allowed Lucy time to talk about how she was feeling. John was extremely supportive both emotionally and physically, holding her hand throughout. The main issues for Lucy were in dealing with her feelings of resentment towards the children, and understanding both her own and John's role in the family. I began by reassuring Lucy that her feelings of resentment were perfectly normal and common in new stepfamilies. The feelings are due to a lack of clarity over roles and responsibilities in the home, and generally reduce over time as couples work together to develop their own roles. We talked about the significant changes that the couple had lived through in the past two years since meeting. Lucy had effectively left behind her single life and become a parent to three children. The children had had to accept Lucy as part of their family and she had clearly done a great job in becoming accepted by them, building good solid relationships. Both John and Lucy were able to see this and recognise how far they had come in a relatively short time.

We then moved on to discuss the issue of discipline. I asked John and Lucy what had been agreed between them and how they handled any bad behaviour from the children. Here, there was clearly a mismatch between the couple. While John expected Lucy to effectively take on the role of 'mother' to the children, Lucy felt this was not agreed and she resented being expected to take on certain aspects of this role – particularly the discipline. While the children were generally not naughty, she didn't feel comfortable in being the person responsible for discipline, however if she didn't deal with this, then she felt John would not address the issues effectively. John understood Lucy's views but felt that as she was 'so good at it' he couldn't understand the problem and therefore felt this was just about giving her more confidence as a new parent. This seemed to frustrate Lucy – she recognised that she was able to fulfil this role but it wasn't what she wanted or felt comfortable with. At this point we were nearing the end of the session and I felt it would be useful for them to go home and consider their roles in the family. I gave them some literature on possible roles for the stepparent and asked them to discuss how these might work with their family dynamics.

In the second session we continued by talking about the roles for Lucy. John clearly felt that she had effectively taken on the role of a third parent, or even replacement mother, while Lucy was uncomfortable with this, preferring to adopt a more friendship-based role, at least in the short term. She didn't want to lead on discipline, expecting John to do this and for her to support him. It was clear that in his relationship with his ex wife, he had not taken on this role and was therefore not entirely comfortable either. I explained to both of them that research consistently shows that it is preferable to let the biological parent lead on discipline in the early stages of the relationship, with the stepparent taking on more responsibility, as they feel more confident in their role and in the family. This seemed to be a difficult issue for the couple, with John failing to understand Lucy's perspective. In his view, she coped extremely well with the children, had developed great relationships with all of them and so it would seem natural that she fell into a more maternal role.

Given the newness of their relationship and the lack of unique issues in the family I thought it might be appropriate for them to attend a group workshop. Lucy's sense of isolation was significant and I felt meeting others in a similar situation would really help her and John to recognise both the positives in their relationship (with each other and with the children) and the common issues of role definition and resentment.

Both agreed that they would be willing to try a group session and this was set up for later that month. Lucy and John attended a day-long workshop that covered all the common stepfamily issues, including roles and responsibilities, normalising stepfamily experiences, strengthening the couple relationship, learning to cope more effectively with the issues, family integration and the importance of a wide circle of support. Both found the workshop incredibly helpful and informative. Lucy was visibly upset at the end of the day, but told me it was tears of relief that she was not alone in her feelings. John explained that he had finally understood how and why Lucy felt the way she did, after hearing from other stepmothers. Previously he recognised that he had simply not wanted to accept that there were any difficulties, expecting

Lucy to take on the full parental role over time. He now recognised that he needed to listen to Lucy and let her take a step back, at least until she felt more confident and able to assume a fuller role with the children.

I continued seeing the couple for several more sessions, however they quickly adapted their behaviour and Lucy was able to cope more effectively and enjoy the company of the children much more. John assumed the lead in disciplining the children and, while he didn't find this easy, he recognised that it was more appropriate that he took the lead, giving more time and space for Lucy to grow into her new role.

Stage 4: Homework

As discussed, Lucy and John were given material to discuss between sessions, related to their difficulties. They were given some definitions of role models, together with the benefits and difficulties of these roles. Having a structure on which to base their discussions allowed them to return to the sessions with more understanding of what they each wanted for their family.

Current situation

Lucy and John continued to thrive as a couple and a stepfamily. Lucy felt more empowered after the sessions and workshop, recognising that her feelings were normal and expected. The following year saw a new addition to the family, a little boy called Kit, and everything continued to go well. However, a year later John contacted me to say that their relationship with his middle child, Cara, had deteriorated. She was refusing to visit John and Lucy, blaming John for leaving her mum. Her behaviour had become difficult for them to handle, with her refusal to accept any rules or discipline in their home. Her school work was suffering and her behaviour there was also a cause for concern. However, her mum refused to believe there was a serious problem, suggesting that this was just typical teenage behaviour. John was becoming more frustrated as he felt unable to resolve the situation.

I set up further sessions with John and Lucy, who needed help in terms of strengthening their own relationship and a strategy for helping John's daughter. The priority was clearly to get support for Cara, however with the biological parents unable to agree on the severity of the problem, a series of mediation sessions were organised between them.

During these sessions the couple agreed that it was important that Cara was encouraged to re-establish her relationship with her father, and to understand the issues behind her change in behaviour and attitude at school. Cara subsequently started seeing a therapist who has helped her establish a healthy relationship with both parents. She has started to visit John and Lucy again, however the relationship is still fragile and the therapy is continuing. During this process I have continued to provide support to John and Lucy, to ensure that their own relationship and the relationships with the other children were not unduly affected during this difficult period.

Conclusion and key learning points

The case studies presented in this chapter provide a wide range of examples of how therapists can approach the broad challenges experienced by stepfamilies. The issues generally fall into common categories and therapists can therefore adopt reasonably standard approaches. However, it is important to recognise the different types of stepfamily as this frequently affects the experiences of the stepparents, and hence all relationships within the family.

Thinking of my own experience and extensive work with stepfamilies, I would urge professionals to consider the different approaches and interventions described within this book. Therapy with the couple is clearly a key component, however support from peers in the form of group workshops is an incredibly valuable tool when used appropriately. Stepfamily couples seeking therapy are at a further disadvantage from biological couples, with ongoing issues related to co-parenting. Often the absent biological parent has no compelling reason to improve their relationship with their ex. However, in cases where there is ongoing conflict, mediation can provide a real benefit for both the stepfamily members and the absent biological parent. If the therapist can act as a catalyst for this it will often help significantly in the development of the stepfamily.

8 CONCLUSION: MAKING A DIFFERENCE

Stepfamilies are now the fastest-growing family type in the UK, yet targeted support is still relatively rare to find. My own experience, derived over the past 10 years, has suggested that blended families are all too frequently offered support that is designed for biological families. Parenting programmes, for example, are designed to help couples feel more confident and deal more effectively with their own biological children. This is not what stepfamilies are typically looking for, or need. The priority for couples in stepfamilies is to find advice that helps them begin to lay down the foundations of their new family unit, to understand their individual roles in the family and to begin to develop solid relationships with all family members. Only when this has been achieved are they ready for more traditional parenting programmes. Unfortunately even couples that seek more traditional one-to-one therapy via counsellors and therapists are sometimes not given the tailored support they need as the professionals fail to recognise the unique nature of the stepfamily dynamic.

The aim of this book has been therefore to explain the unique nature and needs of stepfamilies, and to propose an integrated framework that is firmly rooted in research, theory and practice.

Chapter 1 sought to introduce and explain the premise of the book. What is a stepfamily and why do family professionals need to consider stepfamilies as inherently different to other family types? Why can they not simply be offered the same support and interventions as biological families? Only recently I received a call from a woman whose partner has a child from a previous relationship. She began by apologising as she said she realised she wasn't a stepmum as they weren't married. This example illustrates a very simple and common issue. If we can't even define a stepfamily how can we hope to provide consistent and effective support?

Stepfamilies are, by their nature and makeup, unique among family types. Unlike biological partners, the step-couple relationship was formed after the parent–child relationship. Consequently, the biological parent can often feel torn between loyalty to their children and their new partner. This inherently places additional strains on both relationships and also increases the difficulty for stepparents building a relationship with their stepchildren. The couple also has to maintain links with ex partners in order to co-parent their children. Here biological parents have to maintain a difficult balance: while trying to develop their new relationship they have to negotiate and maintain a working relationship with their ex partner. Often these relationships are fraught with ongoing anger and bitterness, however – paradoxically – if they manage to keep this relationship positive and free from conflict, the relationship with their new partner suffers, with stepparents feeling excluded and resentful of the old ties and ongoing relationship. While there are social norms and expectations for parental roles, roles for stepparents are less clear. Often there is confusion between a couple on the role of the stepparent, with biological parents having differing expectations of their partner and their role in the new family unit. This can lead to further conflict between the couple as they negotiate and clarify their roles.

There are also a number of differences between biological and stepfamilies that relate to the children. Following separation or divorce, children usually continue to see both parents. When one or both of their biological parents re-partners, the children find themselves members of two distinct family groups, with different rules and different members. Children have to negotiate these changes, which can be complex and difficult. Their order in the family can change between the households and children are faced with loyalty conflicts, particularly between their biological parents and stepparents. This can make it difficult for them to build relationships with stepparents as they remain fearful of hurting or upsetting their absent biological parent.

Finally, in terms of the family unit, there are stark differences between the family types. Stepfamilies by their nature form instantly once the adult couple forms a relationship. In biological families, the relationships develop slowly and naturally over time as the family grows. Stepfamilies have no shared history or tradition from which to draw strength, making them more fragile. The relationships that exist within stepfamilies do so only due to the couple relationship. Once this is fractured the individuals are no longer bound together through formal relationships. In addition to relationship complexities, the couple also has to navigate further issues related to shared care of the children, and inevitably financial discussions. Many decisions that biological families make all the time – when to go on holiday, where to spend Christmas, visits to relatives – are simply not straightforward in stepfamilies. The financial implications can also be far reaching, affecting significant decisions in the new family.

Chapter 2 moved on to argue that we need to consider different types of stepfamily as their needs and issues can be diverse. We tend to use the term stepfamily generically, but the reality is that there are several common stepfamily types, each with their own challenges and issues. However, it is possible to segment stepfamilies across two dimensions and independently of the formal relationship between the couple: their complexity, based on whether one adult or both bring children from previous relationships, and the residency of the children, based on whether the children live predominantly with the family or simply come to visit. Research has suggested that families in each of these segments often share common issues. By understanding these, practitioners can be better prepared to offer targeted support and advice. Recognising the attributes of each stepfamily type is also extremely useful for the families themselves. In understanding the key challenges they are thus better prepared to address them and so move on with the next stage of development. It normalises their feelings, allowing them to accept negative feelings and understand why they are experiencing them.

The first two chapters thus provide a backdrop and justification to the integrated therapy described in the following chapters. Chapter 3 introduces the three components that comprise Integrated Stepfamily Therapy (IST), namely couple counselling, psycho-education and behaviour modelling, and mediation. Together these form the foundation of therapy targeted at stepfamilies, allowing for a range of needs and preferences. These can each be used independently or in conjunction with one of the other two approaches in order to deliver the most effective support to the stepfamily. IST has been developed through extensive research and practice, and should build on the existing skills of therapists and counsellors.

Table 8.1 Key principles of Integrated Stepfamily Therapy (IST)

1. If stepfamily-related issues are addressed, the family will be able to move on independently with the development of the family unit.
2. Stepfamilies need solution-focused support to help them cope with the issues related to stepfamily development. Given sufficient and appropriate support, couples will be able to deal effectively with the issues they face.

Thus the principles of IST (see Table 8.1) help guide the resultant therapy, which needs to be specific and focused on the stepfamily-related difficulties. For example, the majority of stepfamily couples arriving at therapy are embarrassed and ashamed of their feelings. They may feel resentful towards their stepchildren, jealous of their partner's ex or angry at the financial settlement. IST helps them realise that these feelings, while not healthy for their relationship in the long term, are both normal and to be expected; rather than suppressing these feelings, they can then work effectively with the practitioner to find alternative ways of coping and dealing with the stressors. It is also important for couples to hold realistic expectations as to the development of their new family. This allows them time and space to develop relationships naturally and without forcing the pace. Often couples have spent all their time and energy in ensuring the children are coping well, without considering the impact on their own relationship. Forcing them to consider this and encouraging them to spend time together, without the children, strengthens the couple bond and in turn helps them cope with the demands from the family. Working out clear roles for stepparents is also essential and often not something that couples have spent any time considering. Yet, without due consideration, this is an area fraught with difficulty due to the differing expectations of both adults. Often parents expect the stepparent to simply step up to the parental role, whereas stepparents often want to take more of a back seat, particularly in the early stages of a relationship. Finally, the biological parent's relationship with their ex is something that needs to have clear boundaries if it is to work effectively and not impact negatively on current relationships.

Chapter 4 introduced the approach to couple counselling within IST. The initial assessment should follow similar principles, which practitioners are already familiar with, such as the use of genograms and a comprehensive understanding of the family background. However, it also requires stepfamily-specific background data to be considered and gathered. Identification of the key problems encourages the client to focus on the particular issues they feel are preventing them from moving on in the family development and integration. It is therefore essential that the practitioner work with the couple to correctly identify the current barriers in order to facilitate progress. The therapeutic work begins in the third stage of the model and may be supported by asking the couple to complete additional tasks outside of the session as a form of homework and a way of re-emphasising the discussion points made in the counselling session. This may take the form of additional reading, further discussion between themselves or completion of other activities. A number of tools are provided within the chapters that professionals can use with clients to support the therapy.

Chapter 5 introduced the topic of psycho-education and behaviour modelling. This form of intervention allows a range of delivery methods, and practitioners are encouraged to consider alternative ways of reaching couples earlier on in their relationships when they have yet to reach crisis point. This approach helps couples cope more effectively with stepfamily stresses by first normalising their experiences and then providing a framework on which to build and develop their new family. Psycho-education suggests that this is merely 'providing information', however that is far from the case. Professionals need to use their experience to help the couple identify the issues preventing further family development, and then use tools and education to help them address these specific difficulties. It is important to recognise that, frequently, stepparents will have been dealing with negative feelings for some time, often having been unable to share these with their partners.

> I know I'm supposed to love my stepchildren, but I don't.

> I feel really resentful when his kids come to stay, but I can't tell him that can I?

> I feel like the outsider in my own home when they come to visit.

> I know I should just deal with it – I am the adult after all. Why do I feel this way?

The above quotes were taken from interviews with stepmums for my own research more than 10 years ago and have been repeated many, many times by clients who have come to see me over the past years.

Offering information and support to these clients, either in a one-to-one or group environment, allows practitioners to normalise their feelings and relieve them of their guilt and shame. Often this frees them to concentrate on the practicalities of developing and integrating their family, and encourages them to seek advice on dealing with their feelings more effectively. For example, if a stepparent feels like an outsider when their partner's children come to stay, how might they change this? What activities could they share and take part in together? Can their partner help in encouraging the children to be more inclusive? Often small changes in the behaviour of the adults can make real improvements in the dynamics within the family.

> We've been together two years and things are just not improving – in fact they're getting worse!

I think I must have heard the above said hundreds of times in my work with stepfamilies! Couples are eternally optimistic in their expectations of family development and hearing that they will need much more time together in order to feel confident as a family often helps them relax and stop putting themselves under too much pressure. Practitioners can then help couples prioritise the steps towards better integration, whether that is needed in their relationship with the children, their own relationship or even in building a better relationship with ex partners.

Chapter 6 introduced the topic of mediation with stepfamilies. At the time of writing, the UK government has just introduced the Children and Families Bill, which ensures that all separating and divorcing couples consider mediation as an alternative to the legal route and courts. All couples that apply for a court order related to their children must therefore first attend a mediation information and assessment meeting (MIAM). The government's own statistics show that the costs of resolving disputes following relationship breakdowns is vastly reduced when mediation is used, as is the time needed to find agreement. In 2013, 17,000 people successfully used publicly funded mediation, with only 6 per cent needing further legal services, compared to 21 per cent of those who didn't use mediation. The shift in focus to the use of mediation with relationship breakdown will, it is hoped, reduce the ongoing conflict between couples that share the ongoing care of their joint children. In turn, this should benefit stepfamilies, as couples are able to co-parent more effectively. However, at present, many stepfamily couples seeking support from professionals are struggling to deal with issues primarily related to ex partners. It is therefore extremely difficult, if not impossible, to support the step couple in isolation from the other biological parent. Having used this intervention in association with conventional couple support and psycho-education, I believe it is an essential tool in the armoury of professionals working with blended families.

Chapter 7 provided a range of case studies, illustrating the different types of stepfamily, together with the range of presenting problems and potential interventions. I have tried to provide examples of different stepfamily types, using a range of interventions, which will hopefully help practitioners when they work with stepfamily clients.

The dynamics of stepfamily relationships only expand the complexity and difficulties experienced by biological families. Whether you are a professional or a stepfamily member I hope that what you have learned from this book will help you understand and accept the differences and challenges that stepfamilies face. Understanding puts us on the right road to dealing with and addressing the problems. Every blended family has its own set of complex relationships, together with its own strengths and difficulties. I have tried to convey both the uniqueness of these families and the recurring, common challenges. Although all stepfamilies (almost without exception!) will face unique difficulties in their journey, they can and do meet these challenges and, with time, patience and understanding, go on to form satisfying and happy family units.

REFERENCES

Adler-Baeder, F. (2001). *Smart Steps: For adults and children in stepfamilies*. Lincoln, NE: Stepfamily Association of America.

Adler-Baeder, F. and Higginbotham, B. (2004). Implications for remarriage and stepfamily formation for marriage education. *Family Relations*, 53, 448–458.

Afifi, T. D. and Schrodt, P. (2003). Uncertainty and the avoidance of the state of one's family in stepfamilies, post-divorce single-parent families, and first-marriage families. *Human Communication Research*, 29(4), 516–532.

Ahrons, C. R. and Wallisch, L. (1987). Parenting in the binuclear family: Relationships between biological and stepparents. In K. Pasley and M. Ihinger-Tallman (eds) *Remarriage and stepparenting: Current research and theory*. New York, NY: Guilford Press, 225–256.

Ambert, A. (1986). Being a stepparent: Live-in and visiting stepchildren. *Journal of Marriage and the Family*, 48, 795–804.

Ambert, A. (2005). *Same sex couples and same sex parent families: Relationships, parenting and issues of marriage*. Ottawa: The Vanier Institute of the Family.

Amato, P. R. (2000). The consequences of divorce for adults and children. *Journal of Marriage and Family*, 62(4), 1269–1287.

Australian Bureau of Statistics (ABS) (1998). *Family characteristics, Australia*. No. 4442.0. Canberra: Author.

Australian Bureau of Statistics (ABS) (2004). *Family characteristics, Australia*. No. 4442.0. Canberra: Author.

Bandura, A. (1977). *Social learning theory*. Englewood Cliffs, NJ: Prentice Hall.

Barrett, A. E. and Turner, R. J. (2005). Family structure and mental health: The mediating effects of socioeconomic status, family process and social stress. *Journal of Health and Social Behaviour*, 46, 156–169.

Beaudry, M., Parent, C., Saint-Jacques, M., Guay, S. and Boisvert, J. (2001). Validation of a questionnaire to assess the difficulties of couples in stepfamilies. *Journal of Divorce and Remarriage*, 35(1/2), 155–172.

Beer, W. R. (1992). *American stepfamilies*. New Brunswick, NJ: Transaction.

Belsky, J. (1984). The determinants of parenting: A process model. *Child Development*, 55, 83–96.

Berger, R. (1998). *Stepfamilies: A multi-dimensional perspective*. New York: Haworth Press.

Berman, C. (1980). *Making it as a stepparent: New roles/new rules*. Garden City, NY: Doubleday.

Bernstein, A. C. (1989). *Yours, mine and ours*. New York: Norton.

Booth, A. and Edwards, J. N. (1992). Starting over: Why remarriages are more unstable. *Journal of Family Issues*, 13(2), 179–194.

Boss, P. (1980a). Normative family stress: Family boundary changes across the life span. *Family Relations*, 29, 445–450.

Boss, P. (1980b). The relationship of psychological father presence, wife's personal qualities and wife/family dysfunction in families of missing fathers. *Journal of Marriage and the Family*, 42(3), 541–549.

Boss, P. (1987). Family stress. In M. B. Sussman and S. K. Steinmetz (eds) *Handbook of marriage and family*. New York: Plenum, 695–723.

Boss, P. and Greenberg, J. (1984). Family boundary ambiguity: A new variable in family stress theory. *Family Process*, 23, 535–546.

Bray, J. H. and Berger, S. H. (1993). Developmental issues in stepfamilies research project: Family relationships and parent–child interactions. *Journal of Family Psychology*, 7(1), 76–90.

Bray, J. and Kelly, J. (1998). *Stepfamilies: Love, marriage and parenting in the first decade*. New York: Broadway.

Brown, G. W., Harris, T. O. and Hepworth, C. (1994). Life events and endogenous depression: A puzzle re-examined. *Archives of General Psychiatry*, 51(7), 525–534.

Brown, K. (1987). Stepmothering: Myth and realities. *Affilia*, 2(4), 34–45.

Bullard, L., Wachlarowicz, M., DeLeeuw, J., Snyder, J., Low, S., Forgatch, M. and DeGarmo, D. (2010). Effects of the Oregon Model of Parent Management Training (PMTO) on marital adjustment in new stepfamilies: A randomized trial. *Journal of Family Psychology*, 24, 485–496.

Bumpass, L. L., Raley, R. K. and Sweet, J. A. (1995). The changing character of stepfamilies: Implications of cohabitation and nonmarital childbearing. *Demography*, 32(3), 425–436.

Burgoyne, J. and Clarke, D. (1984). *Making a go of it: A study of stepfamilies in Sheffield*. London: Routledge & Kegan Paul.

Burt, M. S. and Burt, R. B. (1996). *Stepfamilies: The Step by Step Model of Brief Therapy*. New York: Psychology Press.

Buunk, B. P. and Mutsaers, W. (1999). The nature of the relationship between remarried individuals and former spouses and its impact on marital satisfaction. *Journal of Family Psychology*, 13(2), 165–174.

Cancian, M. and Meyer, D. (1998). Who gets custody? Custody of children in broken families. *Demography*, 35, 147–158.

Cherlin, A. (1978). Remarriage as an incomplete institution. *American Journal of Sociology*, 84, 634–650.

Cherlin, A. and Furstenberg, F. F. Jr. (1994). Stepfamilies in the United States: A reconsideration. *Annual Review of Sociology*, 20, 359–381.

Cherlin, A. J. (2008). Multiple partnerships and children's wellbeing. *Family Matters*, 80, 31–34.

Chorpita, B. F. and Barlow, D. H. (1998). The development of anxiety: The role of control in the early environment. *Psychological Bulletin*, 124(1), 3–21.

Christian, A. (2005). Contesting the myth of the 'wicked stepmother': Narrative analysis of an online stepfamily support group. *Western Journal of Communication*, 69, 27–47.

Church, E. (1999). Who are the people in your family? Stepmothers' diverse notions of kinship. *Journal of Divorce and Remarriage*, 31(1-2), 83–105.

Clarke, S. C. and Wilson, B. F. (1994). The relative stability of remarriages: A cohort approach using vital statistics. *Family Relations*, 43(3), 305–310.

Clements, M. L., Stanley, S. M. and Markman, H. J. (2004). Before they said 'I do': Discriminating among marital outcomes over 13 years. *Journal of Marriage and Family*, 66(3), 613–626.

Clingempeel, W. G. (1981). Quasi kin relationships and marital quality in stepfather families. *Journal of Personality and Social Psychology*, 41, 890–901.

Clingempeel, G., Colyar, J. and Hetherington, E. M. (1994). Toward a cognitive dissonance conceptualisation of stepchildren and biological children loyalty conflicts. A construct validity study. In K. Pasley and M. Ihinger-Tallman (eds) *Stepparenting: Issues in theory, research and practice*. Westport CT: Greenwood, 151–174.

Clingempeel, W. G. and Brand. E. (1985). Structure complexity, quasi kin relationships, marital quality in stepfamilies: A replication, extension and clinical implications. *Family Relations*, 34, 401–409.

Clingempeel, W. G., Brand, E. and Ievoli, R. (1984). Stepparent–stepchild relationships in stepmother and stepfather families. A multimethod study. *Family Relations*, 33, 465–473.

Crosbie-Burnett, M. and Helmbrecht, L. (1993). A descriptive empirical study of gay male stepfamilies. *Family Relations*, 42, 256–62.

Cummings, N. (1990). Brief intermittent psychotherapy throughout the life cycle. In J. K. Zeig and S. G. Gilligan (eds) *Brief therapy: Myths, methods, and metaphors*. New York: Brunner/Mazel Publishers, 169–184.

Dahl, A. S., Cowgill, K. M. and Asmundsson, R. (1987). Life in remarriage families. *Social Work*, 32, 40–44.

de Jong, P. and Berg, I. K. (1998). *Interviewing for solutions*. Pacific Grove, CA: Brooks/Cole.

de Shazer, S. (1985). *Keys to solution in brief therapy*. New York: Norton.

de Vaus, D. (2004). *Diversity and change in Australian families: Statistical profiles*. Melbourne, Victoria: Australian Institute of Family Studies.

De'Ath, E. (1997). Stepfamily policy from the perspective of a stepfamily organisation. *Marriage and Family Review*, 26(3/4), 265–279.

Decker, P. and Nathan, B. (1985) *Behavior modelling training*. New York: Praeger.

Doodson, L. (2014). Understanding the factors related to stepmother anxiety: A qualitative approach. *Journal of Divorce and Remarriage*, 55(8), 645–667.

Doodson, L. J. and Davies, A. P. C. (2014). Different challenges, different well-being: A comparison of psychological well-being across stepmothers and biological mothers and across four categories of stepmothers. *Journal of Divorce and Remarriage*, 55(1), 49–63.

Economic and Social Research Council (2004). *The seven ages of man and woman*. Swindon: Economic and Social Research Council.

Emery, R. E., Matthews, S. G. and Wyer, M. M. (1991). Child custody mediation and litigation: Further evidence on the differing views of mothers and fathers. *Journal of Consulting and Clinical Psychology*, 59(3), 410–418.

Emery, R. E., Sbarra, D. and Grover, T. (2005). Divorce mediation: Research and reflections. *Family Court Review*, 43(1), 22–37.

Emery, R. E., Laumann-Billings, L., Waldron, M. C., Sbarra, D. A. and Dillon, P. (2001). Child custody mediation and litigation: Custody, contact, and coparenting 12 years after initial dispute resolution. *Journal of Consulting and Clinical Psychology*, 69, 323–332.

Erera-Weatherley, P. I. (1996). On becoming a stepparent: Factors associated with the adoption of alternative stepparenting styles. *Journal of Divorce and Remarriage*, 25(3/4), 155–174.

Ferri, E. and Smith, K. (1998). *Stepparenting in the 1990s*. London: Family Policy Studies Centre.

Fine, M. A. (1995) The clarity and content of the stepparent role. A review of the literature. *Journal of Divorce and Remarriage*, 24(1/2), 19–34.

Fine, M. A. and Schwebel, A. I. (1991). Stepparent stress. A cognitive perspective. *Journal of Divorce and Remarriage*, 17, 1–15.

Fine, M. A., Coleman, M. and Ganong, L. H. (1998). Consistency in perceptions of the step-parent role among step-parents, parents and stepchildren. *Journal of Social and Personal Relationships*, 15(6), 810–828.

Forgatch, M. S. and DeGarmo, D. S. (1999). Parenting through change: An effective prevention program for single mothers. *Journal of Consulting and Clinical Psychology*, 67(5), 711–724.

Forste, R. and Heaton, T. B. (2004). The divorce generation: Well-being, family attitudes, and socioeconomic consequences of marital disruption. *Journal of Divorce and Remarriage*, 41, 95–114.

Furstenberg, F. F. and Nord, C. W. (1985). Parenting apart: Patterns of childrearing after marital disruption. *Journal of Marriage and the Family*, 47, 893–905.

Ganong, L. H. and Coleman, M. (1988). Do mutual children cement bonds in stepfamilies? *Journal of Marriage and the Family*, 50(3), 687–698.

Ganong, L., Coleman, M., Fine, M. and Martin, P. (1999). Stepparents' affinity-seeking and affinity-maintaining strategies with stepchildren. *Journal of Family Issues*, 20, 299–327.

Gartrell, N. and Bos, H. M. W. (2010). The US National Longitudinal Lesbian Family Study: Psychological adjustment of 17-year-old adolescents. *Pediatrics*, 126, 1–9.

Gelatt, V. A., Adler-Baeder, F. and Seeley, J. R. (2010). An interactive web-based programme for stepfamilies: Development and evaluation of efficacy. *Family Relations*, 59(5), 572–586.

Gottman, J. and Silver, N. (1999). *The seven principles for making marriage work*. New York: Three Rivers Press, Crown Publishers imprint.

Gottman, J., Levenson, R. W., Swanson, C., Swanson, K., Tyson, R. and Yoshimoto, D. (2003). Observing gay, lesbian and heterosexual couples' relationships: Mathematical modeling of conflict interactions. *Journal of Homosexuality*, 45(1), 65–91.

Halford, K., Nicholson, J. and Sanders, M. (2007). Couple communications in stepfamilies. *Family Process*, 46, 471–483.

Halford, K. W., Markman, H. J., Kline, G. H. and Stanley, S. M. (2003). Best practice in couple relationship education. *Journal of Marital and Family Therapy*, 29, 385–406.

Harwood, K., McLean, N. and Durkin, K. (2007). First time mothers' expectations of parenthood: What happens when optimistic expectations are not matched by later experiences? *Developmental Psychology*, 43(1), 1–12.

Hetherington, E. M. (1993). An overview of the Virginia Longitudinal Study of Divorce and Remarriage with a focus on early adolescence. *Journal of Family Psychology*, 7, 39–56.

Hetherington, E. M. and Kelly, J. (2002). *For better or worse: Divorce reconsidered*. New York: Norton.

Hetherington, E. M., Cox, M. and Cox, R. (1982). Effects of divorce on parents and children. In M. E. Lamb (ed.) *Non-traditional families: Parenting and child development*. Hillsdale, NJ: Lawrence Erlbaum, 233–288.

Higginbotham, B., Davis, P., Smith, L., Dansie, L., Skogrand, L. and Reck, K. (2012). Stepfathers and stepfamily education. *Journal of Divorce and Remarriage*, 53, 76–90.

Higginbotham, B., Skogrand, L. and Torres, E. (2010). Stepfamily education: Perceived benefits for children. *Journal of Divorce and Remarriage*, 51, 36–49.

Higginbotham, B. J. and Adler-Baeder, F. (2008). The 'Smart Steps, Embrace the Journey' program: Enhancing relational skills and relationship quality in remarriages and stepfamilies. *Forum for Family and Consumer Issues*, 13(3).

Hobart, C. (1991). Conflict in remarriages. *Journal of Divorce and Remarriage*, 15(3/4), 69–86.

Ingoldsby, B. B., Smith, S. R. and Miller, J. E. (2004). *Exploring family theories*. Los Angeles, CA: Roxbury.

Johnson, A. J., Wright, K. B., Craig, E. A., Gilchrist, E. S., Lane, L. T. and Haigh, M. M. (2008). A model for predicting stress levels and marital satisfaction for stepmothers utilising a stress and coping approach. *Journal of Social and Personal Relationships*, 25(1), 119–142.

Jones, A. C. (2004). Transforming the story: Narrative applications to a stepmother support group. *Families in Society: The Journal of Contemporary Social Services*, 85, 129–138.

Keeton, C. P., Perry-Jenkins, M. and Sayer, A. G. (2008). Sense of control predicts depressive and anxious symptoms across the transitions to parenthood. *Journal of Family Psychology*, 22(2), 212–221.

Kelly, J. (2004). Family mediation research: Is there empirical support for the field? *Conflict Resolution Quarterly*, 22(1–2), 3–35.

Kelly, J. B. and Gigy, L. (1989). Divorce mediation: Characteristics of clients and outcomes. In K. Kressel and D. Pruitt (eds) *Mediation research: The process and effectiveness of third-party intervention*. San Francisco, CA: Jossey-Bass.

Knox, D. and Zusman, M. E. (2001). Marrying a man with 'baggage': Implications for second wives. *Journal of Divorce and Remarriage*, 35(3-4), 67–79.

Kreider, R. M. (2003). *Adopted children and stepchildren 2000*. Census 2000 Special Reports. US Census 2000.

Kreider, R. M. and Fields, J. (2005). Living arrangements of children: 2001. *Household Economic Studies*. US Census Bureau: Washington, DC, 70–104.

Kurdek, L. A. (1989). Relationship quality for newly married husbands and wives: Marital history, stepchildren, and individual-difference predictors. *Journal of Marriage and the Family*, 51(4), 1053–1064.

Kurdek, L. A. (2004). Are gay and lesbian cohabiting couples really different from heterosexual married couples? *Journal of Marriage and Family*, 66, 880–900.

Larson, J. H. and Allgood, S. M. (1987). A comparison of intimacy in first married and remarried couples. *Journal of Family Issues*, 8(3), 319–331.

Lawton, J. M. and Sanders, M. R. (1994). Designing effective behavioral family interventions for stepfamilies. *Clinical Psychology Review*, 14(5), 463–496.

Lazarus, R. S. and Folkman, S. (1984). *Stress, appraisal and coping*. New York: Springer.

Lynch, J. (2000). Considerations of family structure and gender composition. The lesbian and gay stepfamily. *Journal of Homosexuality*, 40(2), 81–95.

Lynch, J. M. (2005). Becoming a stepparent in gay/lesbian stepfamilies. *Journal of Homosexuality*, 48(2), 45–60.

MacDonald, W. and DeMaris, A. (1996). Parenting stepchildren and biological children: The effects of stepparent's gender and new biological children. *Journal of Family Issues*, 17, 5–25.

Marsiglio, W. (2004). *Stepdads*. Lanham, MD: Rowman & Littlefield.

McGoldrick, M., Gerson, R. and Petry, S. (2008). *Genograms: Assessment and intervention* (3rd edn). New York: Norton.

Minuchin, S. (1974). *Families and family therapy*. Cambridge, MA: Harvard University Press.

Mirowsky, J. and Ross, C. E. (1999). Well being across the life course. In A. V. Horwitz and T. L. Scheid (eds) *A handbook for the study of mental health: Social contexts, theories and systems*. New York: Cambridge University Press, 328–347.

Moore, S. and Cartwright, C. (2005). Adolescents' and young adults' expectations of parental responsibilities in stepfamilies. *Journal of Divorce and Remarriage*, 43, 109–128.

Morrison, K. and Thompson-Guppy, A. (1985). Cinderella's stepmother syndrome. *Canadian Journal of Psychiatry*, 30, 355–363.

Nadler, J. (1977). The psychological stress of the stepmother. *Dissertation Abstracts International*, 37(10-B), April, 53–67.

Nevis, S. and Watner, E. D. (1983). Conversing about Gestalt couple and family therapy. *Gestalt Journal*, 6(2), 40–50.

Nicholson, J. M. and Sanders, M. R. (1999). Randomised controlled trial of behavioural family intervention for the treatment of child behaviour problems in stepfamilies. *Journal of Divorce and Remarriage*, 30, 1–23.

Nielsen, L. (1999). Stepmothers: Why so much stress? A review of the research. *Journal of Divorce and Remarriage*, 30, 115–148.

O'Connor, T. G. and Insabella, G. M. (1999). Marital satisfaction, relationships and roles. *Monographs for the Society for Research in Child Development*, 64(4), 50–78.

O'Connor, T. G., Hawkins, N., Dunn, J., Thorpe, K. and Golding, J. (1998). Family type and depression in pregnancy: Factors mediating risk in a community sample. *Journal of Marriage and the Family*, 60, 757–770.

Office for National Statistics (ONS) (2001). *Families*. London: ONS.

Office for National Statistics (ONS) (2011). *Families*. London: ONS.

Olsen, C. (1997). *Stepping stones for stepfamilies* (training guide). Manhattan: Kansas State University and Cooperative Extension Service.

Orchard, A. L. and Solberg, K. B. (1999). Expectations of the stepmother's role. *Journal of Divorce and Remarriage*, 31(1–2), 107–123.

Papernow, P. (1993). *Becoming a stepfamily*. San Francisco, CA: Jossey-Bass.

Papernow, P. (1996). *Becoming a stepfamily: Patterns of development in remarried families*. Hillside, NJ: Analytic Press.

Papernow, P. (2013). *Surviving and thriving in stepfamily relationships: What works and what doesn't*. New York: Routledge.

Papernow, P. L. (1984). The stepfamily cycle: An experimental model of stepfamily development. *Family Relations*, 33, 355–363.

Pasley, K. and Ihinger-Tallman, M. (1988). Remarriage and stepfamilies. In C. Chilman, E. Nunnally and F. Cox (eds) *Variant family forms*. Newbury Park, CA: Sage, 204–221.

Pasley, K. and Ihinger-Tallman, M. (1989). Boundary ambiguity in remarriage: Does ambiguity differentiate degree of marital adjustment and integration? *Family Relations*, 38(1), 46–56.

Pasley, K., Rhoden, L., Visher, E. B. and Visher, J. S. (1996). Successful stepfamily therapy: Clients' perspective. *Journal of Marital and Family Therapy*, 22(3), 343–357.

Pearson, J. and Thoennes, N. (1988). Divorce mediation research results. In J. Folberg and A. Milne (eds) *Divorce mediation theory and practice*. New York: Guilford Press.

Pfleger, J. (1947). The wicked stepmother. *A Child Guidance Clinic. Smith College Studies in Social Work*, 3, March.

Pill, C. J. (1990). Stepfamilies: Redefining the family. *Family Relations*, 39, 186–193.

Pruett, M. K., Williams, T. Y., Insabella, G. and Little, T. D. (2003). Family and legal indicators of child adjustment to divorce among families with young children. *Journal of Family Psychology*, 17, 169–180.

Pryor, J. (2008). *The international handbook of stepfamilies. Policy and practice in legal, research and clinical interventions*. Hoboken, NJ: Wiley & Sons.

Ratner, H., George, E. and Iveson, C. (2012). *Solution focused brief therapy: 100 key points and techniques*. London: Routledge.

Sanders, M. R., Gooley, S. and Nicholson, J. (2000). Early intervention in conduct problems with children. Vol. 3. In R. Kosky, A. O'Hanlon, G. Martin and C. Davis (eds) *Clinical approaches in child and adolescent mental health*. Vol. 3. Adelaide: Australian Early Intervention Network for Mental Health in Young People.

Schultz, N. C., Schultz, C. L. and Olson, D. H. (1991). Couple strengths and stressors in complex and simple stepfamilies in Australia. *Journal of Marriage and the Family*, 53(3), 555–564.

Severson, M., Smith, S., Ortega, D. and Pettus, C. (2004). Judicial efficiencies in child custody disputes: Lessons and directions for social worker mediators. *Journal of Divorce and Remarriage*, 40(3), 23–40.

Shapiro, D. H., Schwarz, C. E. and Astin, J. A. (1996). Controlling ourselves, controlling our world: Psychology's role in understanding positive and negative consequences of seeking and gaining control. *American Psychologist*, 51, 1213–1230.

Skogrand, L., Davis, P. and Higginbotham, B. J. (2011). Stepfamily education: A case study. *Contemporary Family Therapy*, 33, 61–70.

Stewart, S. D. (2005). How the birth of a child affects involvement with stepchildren. *Journal of Marriage and the Family*, 67, 461–473.

Stewart, S. D. (2007). *Brave new stepfamilies: Diverse paths toward stepfamily living*. London: Sage.

Strasser, F. and Randolph, P. (2004). *Mediation: A psychological insight into conflict resolution*. London: Continuum International Publishing Group Ltd.

Tzeng, J. M. and Mare, R. D. (1995). Labor market and socioeconomic effects on marital stability. *Social Science Research*, 24, 329–351.

US Census Bureau (2005). *Current population survey: Definitions and explanations*. Washington, DC: US Census Bureau.

US Department of Education, Office of Planning, Evaluation and Policy Development (2010). *Evaluation of evidence based practices in online learning: A meta analysis and review of online learning studies*. Washington, DC: US Department of Education.

Vemer, E., Coleman, M., Ganong, L. H. and Cooper, H. (1989). Marital satisfaction in remarriage: A meta-analysis. *Journal of Marriage and the Family*, 51(3), 713–725.

Visher, E. and Visher, J. (1979). *Stepfamilies*. New York: Brunner/Mazel.

Visher, E. B. and Visher, J. S. (1996). *Therapy with stepfamilies*. Philadelphia, PA: Brunner/Mazel.

Visher, E. B., Visher, J. S. and Pasley, K. (2003). *Remarried families and stepparenting*. In F. Walsh (ed.) *Normal family processes: Growing diversity and complexity* (3rd edn). New York: Guilford.

Weaver, S. E. and Coleman, M. (2005). A mothering but not a mother role: A grounded theory study of the non-residential stepmother role. *Journal of Social and Personal Relationships*, 22(4), August, 477–497.

Weston, C. A. and Macklin, E. D. (1990). The relationship between former-spousal contact and remarital satisfaction in stepfather families. *Journal of Divorce and Remarriage*, 14, 25–47.

White, J. M. and Klein, D. M. (2008). *Family theories* (3rd edn). Thousand Oaks, CA: Sage.

White, L. (1998). Who's counting? Quasi facts and stepfamilies in reports of number of siblings. *Journal of Marriage and the Family*, 60(3), 725–733.

White, L. and Booth, A. (1985). The quality and stability of remarriages. The role of stepchildren. *American Sociology Review*, 50, 689–698.

Whitton, S. W., Nicholson, J. M. and Markman, H. J. (2008). Research on interventions for stepfamily couples: The state of the field. In J. Pryor (ed.) *The international handbook of stepfamilies. Policy and practice in legal, research and clinical interventions*. Hoboken, NJ: Wiley & Sons, 445–484.

Zeig, J. K. and Gilligan, S. G. (eds) (1990). *Brief therapy: Myths, methods, and metaphors*. New York: Brunner/Mazel.

Zimet, G. D., Dahlem, N. W., Zimet, S. G. and Farley, G. K. (1988). The Multidimensional Scale of Perceived Social Support. *Journal of Personality Assessment*, 52(1), 30–41.

INDEX

Page numbers in *italics* refer to figures and tables.

Happy Relationships at Home, Work & Play

Beresford

ISBN: 9780077145910 (Paperback)
eBook: 9780077145927
2013

In this insightful, warmly written book, psychotherapist and Psychologies agony aunt Lucy Beresford cuts to the chase of how to have harmonious, fulfilling relationships. Whether it's with our partner, our kids, our boss or our mother-in-law, or perhaps most importantly ourselves, all our relationships require – at some stage in our lives – a little bit of tender loving care. A helpful toolkit in dealing with everyday dilemmas, it will boost your confidence, encourage insight and empower you to be the best you can be in all your relationships.

www.mheducation.co.uk

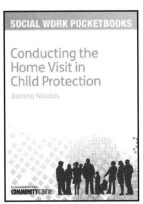

CONDUCTING THE HOME VISIT IN CHILD PROTECTION
Second Edition

Joanna Nicolas

ISBN: 9780335261789 (Paperback)
eBook: 9780335261796

2015

Conducting a home visit is a fundamental part of a social worker's role, which can be overlooked during social work training. This is a practical guide to conducting home visits, a task which many newly qualified social workers can feel unprepared for and which can be fraught with difficulties.

Useful features of this book include:
- Real case examples based on practitioners' experiences
- Realistic solutions to the everyday difficulties you might face
- Examples of what to say
- Reference to the latest guidance, including Working Together to Safeguard Children (2015), to ensure you are practising in line with statutory requirements and expectations.

www.**mheducation**.co.uk

OPEN UNIVERSITY PRESS
McGraw - Hill Education